legalizing
marijuana
promises and pitfalls

MARGARET J. GOLDSTEIN

TWENTY-FIRST CENTURY BOOKS / MINNEAPOLIS

For the Chief, who every day turns Chaos into Control
—99

Twenty-First Century Books
A division of Lerner Publishing Group, Inc.
241 First Avenue North
Minneapolis, MN 55401 USA

For reading levels and more information, look up this title at www.lernerbooks.com.

Main body text set in Conduit ITC Std Light 11/15.
Typeface provided by International Typeface Corp.

Library of Congress Cataloging-in-Publication Data

Names: Goldstein, Margaret J., author.
Title: Legalizing marijuana : promises and pitfalls / Margaret J. Goldstein.
Description: Minneapolis : Twenty-First Century Books, 2016. | Includes bibliographical
     references and index.
Identifiers: LCCN 2016008283 (print) | LCCN 2016008475 (ebook) |
ISBN 9781467792431 (lb : alk. paper) | ISBN 9781512411447 (eb pdf)
Subjects: LCSH: Marijuana—Law and legislation—United States—Juvenile literature. |
     Drug legalization—United States—Juvenile literature.
Classification: LCC KF3891.M2 G65 2016 (print) | LCC KF3891.M2 (ebook) |
     DDC 345.73/0277—dc23

LC record available at http://lccn.loc.gov/2016008283

Manufactured in the United States of America
1-38271-20000-3/7/2016

Contents

1

a new leaf

Matt and Paige Figi of Denver, Colorado, were desperate. Their five-year-old daughter Charlotte had been diagnosed with a rare disease called Dravet syndrome, a severe, life-threatening form of epilepsy. People with epilepsy suffer from large and small seizures, caused by sudden bursts of electrical energy in the brain. During the most severe (grand mal) seizures, patients' muscles jerk and convulse and they lose consciousness. Charlotte had had her first seizure when she was three months old. She was diagnosed with Dravet at the age of two.

To reduce the number and severity of Charlotte's seizures, doctors prescribed powerful pharmaceutical drugs and put her on diets designed to control seizures. The treatments worked only briefly. The seizures always came back after a short period of time. The seizures and the side effects of the drugs took a heavy toll on Charlotte's brain and body. While her twin sister, Chase, learned to walk and talk like other kids their age, Charlotte deteriorated. She couldn't walk, talk, or eat on her own. She was confined to a wheelchair and had to be fed through a tube. She was hospitalized repeatedly, and her heart had stopped several times. By 2012 five-year-old Charlotte was having about three hundred severe seizures per week. Some of them lasted from two to four hours. The condition brought Charlotte close to death. "The doctors told us to prepare for her death—they told us that she wouldn't pull through," said her mother.

But the Figis did not give up hope. Matt Figi spent hours online looking for treatments for Dravet syndrome. During one Internet session, he saw a video about a boy with Dravet whose parents were feeding him oil derived from the cannabis plant, the source of the drug marijuana. After starting on regular doses of the oil, the boy had dramatically fewer seizures.

Matt told his wife about the video and urged that they start Charlotte on a similar treatment. But Paige Figi resisted. She knew that marijuana was a mind-altering drug. "When Matt first told me about the treatment, I was horrified," she recalled. "I didn't want my daughter to get high." But the Figis soon learned that not all marijuana is mind-altering.

Charlotte Figi, seven, walks in a Colorado greenhouse where growers raise a strain of cannabis known as Charlotte's Web. The strain was named for Charlotte, whose severe—and rare—form of epilepsy has been treated successfully with the plant's oil since 2012. Colorado is one of many US states that have legalized medical marijuana.

The boy in the video ingested oil from a strain of cannabis that is very low in tetrahydrocannabinol (THC), the psychoactive (mind-altering) compound that gives marijuana users a feeling of euphoria, known as a high. And the strain is rich in cannabidiol (CBD), a chemical thought to have many medical benefits. The CBD appeared to be quieting the seizure-causing electrical activity in the boy's brain.

Feeling that they had exhausted all other options, the Figis decided to feed the same kind of oil to Charlotte. Several years earlier, in 2000, the state of Colorado had created a program to provide medical marijuana to people suffering from certain kinds of illnesses, such as cancer. To receive medical marijuana, patients had to get specific documents signed by two doctors. But because Charlotte was so young, doctors were reluctant to approve her as a marijuana patient. Finally, the Figis found two local doctors to provide the required signatures, and Charlotte became Colorado's youngest medical marijuana patient. Her first dose of CBD oil had an immediate—and astounding—effect. "When we first gave her the cannabis oil, she went from having hundreds of seizures a day to none. She went for seven days without a twitch. It was unbelievable," Paige said.

By 2013, after a year on CBD oil, six-year-old Charlotte was a changed girl. She had only a few seizures each month, mostly in her sleep. She was walking, talking, riding a bike, eating normally, laughing, and enjoying life. She still physically and mentally lagged behind her sister and other kids their age, but she was catching up quickly. Her father credits the CBD oil with saving her life. "I want to scream it from the rooftops," he told a reporter. "I want other people, other parents [of children who suffer from seizures], to know that this [CBD oil] is a viable option."

LAWS OF THE LAND

The Figis are lucky to live in a state with a medical marijuana program, but Charlotte's marijuana use is part of a much more complicated story. In fact, marijuana is extremely controversial and in many places illegal. Since 1970 the US government has classified marijuana as a Schedule I drug. According to the US Drug Enforcement Administration (DEA), the agency that enforces US drug laws,

> Schedule I drugs, substances, or chemicals are defined as drugs
> with no currently accepted medical use and a high potential
> for abuse. Schedule I drugs are the most dangerous drugs of
> all the drug schedules with potentially severe psychological
> or physical dependence. Some examples of Schedule I drugs
> are: heroin, lysergic acid diethylamide (LSD), marijuana
> (cannabis), 3,4-methylenedioxymethamphetamine (ecstasy),
> methaqualone, and peyote.

Because the federal government considers marijuana such a dangerous drug, people who are caught growing it, selling it, or possessing it can be subject to punishment, including lengthy prison sentences and thousands of dollars in fines, depending on how much marijuana is involved. Every year, about 750,000 Americans are arrested for marijuana offenses.

Yet even though the cultivation, sale, possession, and use of marijuana are illegal under federal law, they are legal under many state laws. By 2015 the District of Columbia (Washington, DC) and twenty-three US states, Colorado among them, had legalized marijuana for medical use. Washington, DC, and four states (Colorado, Alaska, Oregon, and Washington) had legalized marijuana for recreational use. So when the Figis give Charlotte CBD oil to control her seizures, they are acting lawfully in Colorado but are breaking federal law.

According to the Supremacy Clause of the US Constitution, when federal and state laws are in conflict, federal law takes precedence. That clause gives the federal government the power to enforce antimarijuana laws even in states where the drug is legal. For example, when California became the first state to set up a medical marijuana program, in 1996, the federal government was quick to take action. Over the next ten-plus years, DEA agents carried out numerous raids on California medical marijuana operations.

CHARLOTTE'S WEB

Matt and Paige Figi at first had a hard time finding low-THC/high-CBD marijuana for their daughter Charlotte. Then they found the Stanley brothers, owners of a large Colorado marijuana nursery and several dispensaries (offices or clinics where patients can purchase legal medicines). The five brothers had crossbred plants to develop just the type of nonintoxicating cannabis that Charlotte needed. After the Stanleys heard Charlotte's story, they not only supplied CBD oil to the Figis at minimal cost, but they also changed the name of the cannabis strain they had developed to Charlotte's Web, after the spiderweb of a beloved children's book of the same name. What's more, they formed an organization called Realm of Caring to provide CBD oil at low cost to the families of other children suffering from epilepsy.

The demand for Charlotte's Web oil was great, but under Colorado law, the Stanleys were limited in how many cannabis plants they could grow. They were also prohibited from shipping CBD oil out of Colorado. Hundreds of families with epileptic children moved to Colorado from other states to legally buy CBD oil from the Stanleys. By the summer of 2014, the brothers had a waiting list of nine thousand patients who wanted to buy their oil. The families who were able to get the oil reported a massive reduction in their children's seizures, just as the Figis had.

The Stanleys have increased their acreage to grow more Charlotte's Web in Colorado. They are also setting up a growing operation in Uruguay, a South American nation that has legalized marijuana. To comply with Colorado law, the Stanleys have had Charlotte's Web officially reclassified as hemp (another name for the cannabis plant) instead of marijuana. Cannabis containing less than 0.3 percent THC is legally designated as hemp, and a 2014 law allows Colorado farmers to grow hemp with few restrictions.

The Stanleys ship some of their product across state lines. However, the federal government prohibits the interstate sale of all forms of cannabis—whether it's classified as hemp or as marijuana. But the brothers are willing to take that risk. "We are hoping the enforcement agencies have bigger fish to fry and don't want to take a bunch of medicine away from sick kids," said Jared Stanley. "But if they are going to do it, we're all in. If you are going to be locked up, it's a thing worth getting locked up for."

Jon Stanley waters high-CBD cannabis plants, including the Charlotte's Web variety, in the Colorado greenhouse he runs with his brothers.

They arrested many sick people and those who were supplying them with marijuana to ease pain, nausea, and seizures. Because of the Supremacy Clause, these Americans, who had been complying with state law, weren't protected from arrest or prosecution by the federal government.

The situation changed in 2009. In October, during President Barack Obama's first term, the US Department of Justice issued a memo to federal prosecutors. Named the Ogden memo for its issuer, Deputy Attorney General David W. Ogden, the directive said that the department would focus its staff and funding resources on pursuing "significant traffickers of illegal drugs" and that prosecutors should not go after people who complied with existing state medical marijuana laws. "For example," the memo stated, "prosecution of individuals with cancer or other serious illnesses who use marijuana as part of a recommended treatment regimen consistent with applicable state law, or those caregivers in clear and unambiguous compliance with existing state law who provide such individuals with marijuana, is unlikely to be an efficient use of limited federal resources."

The announcement marked a turning point for the movement to legalize medical marijuana. By then thirteen US states had implemented legal medical marijuana programs. Once the federal government declared its new priorities, medical marijuana businesses boomed in states where medical marijuana was already legal. Other states began to follow suit, passing laws to allow for medical marijuana programs. At the same time, however, marijuana remained on the federal government's Schedule I list, classified as a drug with no medical use, a designation that many people wanted to see changed.

THE NEXT STEP

Many Americans use marijuana recreationally. They don't need it to manage medical conditions. They use it because they like how it makes them feel.

But in 2009, Americans who used marijuana recreationally had no choice but to buy it through black market channels—that is, from a network of illegal growers, street dealers, and drug cartels. At that time, many Americans believed that marijuana should be legal for all adults—whether or not they were sick. They based their outlook on studies that have shown that marijuana is far safer than alcohol and tobacco, both of which are legal in the United States. Advocates began arguing for a legal marijuana industry that would be taxed and regulated by the government. Such an industry, they pointed out, would take away business from the illegal—and sometimes violent—black market.

Activists in Colorado and Washington State put forward bills to legalize recreational marijuana for adults (aged twenty-one and over) in their states, and in 2012, voters approved the measures. Both states created strict rules and regulations about marijuana cultivation and sale, and hundreds of marijuana businesses opened their doors to consumers. People watched cautiously to see whether the federal government would step in and shut down these businesses as it had done with medical marijuana operations in California. But President Obama made it clear once again that the federal government had other priorities. In December 2012, he told reporter Barbara Walters,

> [In] Washington and Colorado, you've seen the voters speak on this issue. And as it is, the federal government has a lot to do when it comes to criminal prosecutions. It does not make sense from a prioritization point of view for us to focus on recreational drug users in a state that has already said that under state law that's legal. . . . We're going to need to have a [national] conversation about how do you reconcile a federal law that still says marijuana is a federal offense and state laws that say it's legal.

In August 2013, the US Justice Department followed up with another memo to federal prosecutors. It stressed that in states where marijuana is legal, the federal government will put its emphasis on keeping the drug

In March 2015, employees at Cannabis Corner in North Bonneville, Washington, prepare for their store's grand opening. Cannabis Corner is the first city-owned recreational marijuana retailer in the United States.

out of the hands of minors, preventing drugged driving and other dangers posed by marijuana use, and keeping criminal enterprises out of the marijuana industry.

In November 2014, two additional states, Alaska and Oregon, legalized marijuana for recreational use. A few months later, the city council of Washington, DC, made it legal for district residents to grow up to six marijuana plants at home, for personal marijuana use. In 2014 a Gallup poll found that for the first time, a slight majority of Americans—51 percent—supported marijuana legalization for any use. By October 2015, nationwide support for legalized marijuana for any use was at 58 percent. The United States was entering new territory.

Long demonized in the nation as a "killer weed," marijuana is gaining widespread acceptance.

But many questions remain. How exactly—and how well—does marijuana work to treat different health problems? Will legalization take the marijuana business out of the hands of criminal gangs? How will state governments ensure that young people don't get access to marijuana in states where it is legal for adults? Will the federal government remove marijuana from Schedule I? The American people, along with policy makers, doctors, and law enforcement officials, are pondering these issues as the states and the federal government grapple with the legalization of marijuana.

marijuana comes full circle

Cannabis is a hardy plant, able to thrive in a variety of climates, soils, and altitudes. It grows wild in warm and cool places all over the world. Cannabis is also a useful plant. Its strong, thick stalks can be made into rope, cloth, and paper. Fibers made from cannabis stalks are commonly called hemp, although *hemp* is also a name for the cannabis plant itself. Marijuana consists of the dried leaves and flowers of the cannabis plant. When smoked or eaten, it is an intoxicant, although it is not as strong as hashish, the amber-colored resin produced by the flowers of the female cannabis plant. THC is the psychoactive ingredient in hashish and marijuana—the chemical that makes users who eat or smoke them high. Cannabis seeds contain yellowish-green oil, and in earlier centuries, people used the oil as a lamp fuel and as an ingredient in soap, varnish, and paints. Birds and small animals eat cannabis seeds, and in parts of India and Africa, cooks have long included the seeds in various recipes.

Archaeological and historical records are full of examples of ancient peoples using cannabis to make rope, clothing, paper, food, and medicine. Around 2700 BCE, Chinese emperor Shen Nung wrote about cannabis in a medical book called the *Pen Ts'ao Ching.* He recommended *ma,* or marijuana, for more than one hundred health problems, including gout, malaria, and constipation. He also noted the drug's mind-altering qualities, writing, "If one takes it over a long period of time, one can communicate with spirits, and one's body becomes light." But the emperor also cautioned that when used in excess, *ma* "makes people see demons." Cannabis played a role in ancient religions. In ancient India, for example, holy men smoked hashish and drank bhang, a cannabis-based beverage, to achieve enlightenment—a state of spiritual insight.

This illustration of a cannabis plant is from a guide to medicinal plants written by Greek physician and surgeon Pedanius Dioscorides, who lived in the first century CE. Originally written in Greek, Dioscorides's book was later translated into Latin as *De Materia Medica*.

"A SUBSTANCE OF A HUNDRED OPERATIONS"

Cannabis grew wild in ancient Europe, and people there also used the plant. During the Middle Ages (about 500 to 1500 CE), European healers prescribed cannabis for earaches, toothaches, menstrual pains, labor pains, headaches, coughs, fevers, inflammation, and other ailments. Much of Europe has cool weather, and cannabis native to cool places does not contain as much mind-altering THC as that from hot-weather locales. Therefore, the medical cannabis used by Europeans in the Middle Ages likely did not make them high.

Europeans of earlier centuries also used cannabis to make hempen paper, rope, yarn, and clothing. Fibers made from hemp are durable and salt water-resistant, which made them ideal for sailcloth, fishing nets, and ships' ropes. Italians referred to hemp as "quello delle cento operazioni," or the "substance of a hundred operations."

In the late sixteenth century, Europeans began to establish colonies in North America. The colonists brought their traditions of cannabis use with them from Europe. In colonial Virginia, future US president George Washington grew hemp on his estate. Future president Thomas Jefferson wrote the first draft of the US Declaration of Independence on hemp paper, and the cloth for the first US flags was made of hemp. By the mid-nineteenth century, hemp was the nation's third-largest crop, behind cotton and tobacco.

At that time, British scientists working in India (part of the British Empire) noted the healing powers of Indian-grown cannabis, which contains more THC than European varieties. Soon European and US drug companies were making tinctures (herbal extracts mixed into liquids), tonics, and balms containing Indian hemp. The remedies were sold at apothecary shops, or drugstores. One popular remedy was Squire's Extract, used to relieve nausea, tremors, and muscle spasms. By 1850 cannabis was listed in *United States Pharmacopeia,* a book published by the US Pharmacopeial Convention, a group of physicians who set standards and guidelines for medicines used in the United States.

MIGRATIONS

People in warmer parts of the world used cannabis that was high in TCH. In the Middle East and North Africa, for example, men smoked hashish in bazaars and coffee shops. Arab traders introduced cannabis to sub-Saharan Africa. There the plant was used for religious ceremonies, magic, and medicine. From the seventeenth to the nineteenth centuries, slave traders shipped African captives across the Atlantic Ocean to work on plantations in the Americas. Sailors and slaves brought cannabis seeds with them from West Africa to sugar plantations in Brazil in South America. The plant spread from there to indigenous communities of Mexico and Central America, which used it in religious rituals.

By the 1880s, cannabis was widespread in Mexico. Peasants (poor farmers) grew it on small plots, smoked it in pipes and rolled it into cigarettes, and mixed it into sweet beverages. *Curanderos,* or healers, gave cannabis to their patients. The term *marijuana* (originally spelled *marihuana*) comes from Mexico, although scholars aren't sure of its origin. It might come from the Spanish-language phrase *Maria y Juana* (Mary and Jane), a slang term for a house of prostitution, presumably a place where marijuana was smoked. The Aztec Indian word *mallihuan,* meaning "taken prisoner," is another possible origin.

At the beginning of the twentieth century, a troubled economy and a dictatorial government in Mexico compelled large numbers of Mexican laborers to move north to the United States, many of them to Texas towns along the Rio Grande. These migrants brought marijuana with them. They continued to import the drug from Mexico to Texas, where grocers sold it in their stores.

DREAMS AND NIGHTMARES

In the mid-nineteenth century, smoking hashish—imported from India and the Arab world—became fashionable in Paris, France, especially among writers, artists, and musicians. In 1846 French author Théophile Gautier described his experience with hashish in glowing terms:

> I was experiencing a complete transposition of taste. The water I was drinking seemed to have the savour of the most exquisite wine, the meat turned to raspberries in my mouth, and vice versa. . . . My body seemed to be dissolved and transparent. Within my chest, I clearly saw the hashish I had eaten, like an emerald giving off millions of tiny sparks.

But Gautier also warned readers that before eating hashish, it was "most important to be in a good disposition—both in mind and body," or else "ecstasy may readily turn into nightmare."

Hemp was a major crop in the United States for decades. In this photo from the early 1900s, farmworkers in Kentucky use hand-operated machines to separate hemp fibers from the plant's inner core. Kentucky farms were the major source of American hemp until the Civil War (1861–1865).

STRAIGHT AND NARROW

Until the twentieth century, intoxicating drugs were freely available to US consumers. Many remedies sold in drugstores contained marijuana, opium, or cocaine. Cocaine was also an ingredient in Coca-Cola, the popular soft drink. In 1898 the German chemical company Bayer introduced a drug called heroin as a treatment for pneumonia, tuberculosis, and other respiratory illnesses. But it soon became clear that heroin, which is derived from opium, was dangerously addictive.

In the United States, public health officials began to sound the alarm about the widespread availability of habit-forming and mind-altering drugs. In 1906 Congress passed the Pure Food and Drug Act, which required that medicine makers label any intoxicating ingredients in medicines sold over the counter, or without a doctor's prescription. In 1914 Congress passed the Harrison Narcotics Act, which made cocaine and any drugs derived from opium available only by prescription. Marijuana was not included in the Harrison Narcotics Act, but some local and state governments passed laws forbidding its sale and use. The federal government outlawed heroin altogether in 1924.

The pushback against intoxicating, addictive drugs coincided with a movement to ban the manufacture, sale, and transport of alcoholic beverages in the United States—based on the argument that drunkenness damages health, families, and society. The Eighteenth Amendment to the US Constitution, ratified in 1919, formalized the ban nationwide.

During the Prohibition era, Americans often drank liquor on the sly. This woman kept a flask under her garter.

The effort to eliminate drinking alcoholic beverages, called Prohibition, was largely a failure. Instead of ridding the nation of alcohol use, the Prohibition law forced drinkers, manufacturers, and taverns underground. Criminal gangs took over the liquor business, and Americans drank illegally at secret nightclubs called speakeasies. A vast majority of Americans—including President Warren G. Harding and members of Congress—regularly broke Prohibition laws. In 1933, in response to public pressure and the growing alarm about Prohibition-related crime, US states ratified the Twenty-First Amendment, which repealed Prohibition.

REEFER MADNESS

Through the years of Prohibition, marijuana use endured in Mexican American communities. Meanwhile, jazz music, rooted in African American musical traditions, became popular in cities such as New Orleans, Chicago, and New York. At 1920s jazz shows, African American musicians played vibrant, fast-paced, and heavily syncopated tunes. Although the shows were popular with white audiences, especially in big cities, the unfamiliar, impassioned sounds of jazz alarmed some white commentators. Marijuana was an element of the jazz scene: many jazz musicians smoked—and wrote songs about—the drug.

During this era, racial prejudice and discrimination were rampant, and many Anglo-Americans made associations between marijuana use, racial minorities, jazz music, and amoral behavior. Marijuana became associated with ugly racial stereotypes. "All Mexicans are crazy, and this stuff [marijuana] makes them crazy," declared one Texas state senator.

Harry J. Anslinger, who in 1930 became the first head of the Federal Bureau of Narcotics (FBN), took antimarijuana rhetoric to new heights. Hoping to persuade Congress to better fund his cash-strapped bureau, Anslinger aimed to convince mainstream, white Americans that marijuana was a threat to the nation's youth—a concern that required an aggressive federal response. Anslinger is remembered for a long list of racist, inflammatory, and unproven theories, such as, "There are 100,000 total marijuana smokers in the US, and most are [African Americans], Hispanics, Filipinos and entertainers. Their Satanic music, jazz and swing, result from marijuana usage. This marijuana causes white women to seek sexual relations with [African Americans], entertainers and any others." Anslinger fed the newspapers fantastical tales about marijuana-crazed ax murderers, rapists, and degenerates, writing many of the articles himself. Marijuana was "as dangerous as a coiled rattlesnake," he warned in one piece. Filmmakers joined in with lurid stories of marijuana depravity. The 1936 film *Tell Your Children,* later called *Reefer Madness,* has its marijuana-addled characters jumping out of windows, attempting rape, shooting one another, going insane, and running down pedestrians in cars.

Persuaded by Anslinger's propaganda, many states outlawed marijuana in the 1930s. In April and May 1937, Congress considered legislation

The "Sweet PILL" that MAKES LIFE BITTER!

ADULTS ONLY!

WOMEN CRY FOR IT— MEN DIE FOR IT!

"REEFER MADNESS"

SEE

DRUG-CRAZED ABANDON

YOUTHFUL MARIHUANA VICTIMS

WHAT ACTUALLY HAPPENS!

THE FIRESIGN THEATRE

MARTIAN SPACE PARTY

NOT INSANE

A poster promotes *Reefer Madness,* a cautionary, propagandistic 1936 film about the dangers awaiting young people who use marijuana. French-born Louis Gasnier directed the film, which starred mostly unknown actors. In the 1970s, the movie became a cult hit among marijuana users.

called the Marijuana Tax Act. The bill said that anyone growing, transporting, selling, prescribing, or using marijuana had to register with the government and pay a tax of one dollar per ounce on every business transaction. Those who failed to register were taxed at one hundred dollars per ounce. Anslinger testified before Congress in support of the act, repeating his oft-told tales of the alleged horrors of marijuana. Dr. William C. Woodward, representing the American Medical Association, spoke in opposition to the bill, challenging arguments about marijuana's dangers and saying that, in fact, the drug had medicinal value. Congress disregarded Woodward's testimony, and the bill passed easily.

At that time, marijuana was still an ingredient in various medicines, but the new tax was so high that pharmaceutical companies dropped it from their remedies. In addition, because of changing attitudes and restrictive legislation, in 1942 the US Pharmacopeial Convention dropped marijuana from the *United States Pharmacopeia.* Although marijuana was technically still legal under federal law, the Marijuana Tax Act essentially outlawed the drug by making it far too expensive to buy or sell legally.

Additional US laws—the 1951 Boggs Amendment to the Harrison Narcotics Act and the Narcotics Control Act of 1956—increased prison terms for all narcotics offenses, including marijuana offenses. During congressional hearings for the Boggs Amendment, Harry Anslinger, still head of the FBN, put forth what came to be known as the gateway theory— the unproven speculation that marijuana use leads people to harder, more dangerous, and more addictive drugs. Anslinger told lawmakers, "The danger is this: Over 50 percent of those young [heroin] addicts started on marijuana smoking. They started there and graduated to heroin; they took the needle when the thrill of marijuana was gone."

YOUTH QUAKE

The Eighteenth Amendment had not kept Americans from drinking alcohol, and antidrug laws did not keep them from smoking marijuana. The new harsh sentences for drug offenders—two to five years in prison for possession of marijuana under the Boggs Amendment, for instance— simply made users extremely cautious.

Most white Americans of the 1950s had little knowledge of the African American jazz scene, but in New York City, some nonconformists plunged into this world with gusto. Writers Jack Kerouac, Allen Ginsberg, William S. Burroughs, and their friends—all of them white—broke with social norms, hung out in jazz clubs, and took delight in the free-form sounds of bebop music, an instrumental, improvisational form of jazz. Like many of the jazz players they admired, the writers used marijuana and other illegal drugs recreationally. Their drug-induced experiences often served as inspiration for their writings and other artistic efforts.

The Beats, as the young writers called themselves, broke all the rules of 1950s America. They wrote poems and books about drug use, homosexuality, and other taboo subjects. Many mainstream Americans viewed the Beats with disdain, but some young people were attracted to their message of freedom

A young man and woman share a marijuana cigarette at a 1969 rock concert in San Francisco. Marijuana played a major role in the 1960s counterculture movement of youthful rebellion.

and rebellion. By the early 1960s, inspired in part by the Beats, a small youth movement had begun in the United States. It grew larger and larger as the decade went on.

Young people of the 1960s—especially college students—launched a countercultural movement. They listened to loud, beat-heavy rock-and-roll music, experimented with illegal drugs, and searched to challenge the norms of their parents, the government, and other authority figures. On college campuses, students demonstrated against US involvement in the controversial Vietnam War (1957–1975). Calling themselves hippies, some young people spoke of "flower power," a philosophy of love and nonviolence. While their parents dressed conservatively, in trim suits and neat dresses, with short, styled hairdos, many youths of the 1960s wore colorful, flowing clothing. Young women wore their hair long and free-flowing, and many young men grew long hair and beards. Also during this era, African Americans protested for civil rights and women launched a movement for equality between the sexes.

Marijuana became a symbol of youthful defiance. Bob Dylan, the Beatles, and other popular musicians sang about getting stoned on marijuana. Americans smoked the drug openly during the 1967 Summer of Love, a spontaneous, months-long hippie gathering in San Francisco, and at the 1969 Woodstock music festival in upstate New York. "When a young person took his first puff of psychoactive smoke [marijuana], he also drew in the psychoactive culture as a whole. . . ." said Michael Rossman, a 1960s college activist. "One inhaled a certain way of dressing, talking, acting, certain attitudes. One became a youth criminal against the State [a rebel]."

PUBLIC ENEMY NUMBER ONE

Many traditional Americans looked upon the 1960s youth movement with alarm. They were upset and frightened to see young people getting high on drugs and challenging sexual, social, and political norms. Americans were further disturbed by news that many US soldiers in Vietnam were routinely turning to heroin, marijuana, and other illicit drugs to deal with the horrors of that war.

President Richard Nixon was a voice of social conservatism. In 1969, to calm some of the fears many Americans felt at this time of social upheaval, he launched what came to be called the War on Drugs. To fight marijuana use, for example, the Nixon administration pressured Mexico to outlaw the cultivation of cannabis, which until then had been legal in Mexico and accounted for a significant portion of the nation's agricultural income. The Nixon administration also increased efforts to intercept marijuana shipments along the 1,933-mile (3,111-kilometer) US–Mexico border.

The War on Drugs included the 1970 Comprehensive Drug Abuse and Control Act, which combined a patchwork of federal antidrug laws under one statute (law). A section of the law called the Controlled Substances Act placed each illegal drug into one of five schedules, or categories. Schedule I was reserved for the most dangerous and addictive drugs, including heroin and LSD, a substance that can cause users to hallucinate and lose touch with reality. Marijuana was also placed in Schedule I, although this was a temporary decision, to be reviewed later by a federal commission. Meanwhile, cocaine and opium were placed in Schedule II, a category reserved for drugs that were dangerous and addictive but were thought to have some legitimate medical uses.

Raymond Shafer, then a former governor of Pennsylvania, chaired the National Commission on Marihuana and Drug Abuse, the commission charged with assessing the dangers of marijuana and deciding whether it should remain in Schedule I. Members of the Shafer Commission, as it came to be known, did extensive research on marijuana and interviewed doctors, scientists, and law enforcement officers. Aggressively opposed to drug use and the hippie scene, which he viewed as dangerous threats to national stability, President Nixon pushed the commission to condemn marijuana in its final report. "I want a goddamn strong statement about marijuana," he told Shafer privately.

The commission's 1,184-page report was not at all what the president had expected. Titled *Marihuana: A Signal of Misunderstanding,* the document stated, "Neither the marijuana user nor the drug itself can be said to constitute a danger to public safety." The report recommended the decriminalization of "possession of marijuana for personal use" and the "casual distribution of small amounts of marijuana." The report also recommended further study to investigate marijuana's potential medical benefits. President Nixon ignored the recommendations, and marijuana remained a Schedule I drug.

In 1973 Nixon created the DEA, a federal office tasked with carrying out, in his words, "an all-out global war on the drug menace." The next year, Congress created the National Institute on Drug Abuse to carry out scientific research on drug abuse and drug addiction and to develop policies for preventing and treating them.

"Use of the drug [marijuana] is linked with idleness, lack of motivation, hedonism [extreme pleasure-seeking] and sexual promiscuity. Many see the drug as fostering a counterculture which conflicts with basic moral precepts [principles] as well as with the operating functions of our society. The 'dropping out' or rejection of the established value system is viewed with alarm. Marihuana becomes more than a drug; it becomes a symbol of the rejection of cherished values."

—National Commission on Marihuana
and Drug Abuse report excerpt, March 1972

JUST SAY YES, NO, AND MAYBE

Pro-marijuana forces rallied to counter federal law. The National Organization for the Reform of Marijuana Laws (NORML), formed in 1970, lobbied federal and state legislatures for the legalization of marijuana. *High Times,* a magazine that celebrates marijuana use, was launched in 1974. Working in secret, marijuana growers crossbred plants to create strains with ever-higher amounts of THC.

In 1978 President Jimmy Carter, a Democrat and much more socially liberal than Nixon, sent an encouraging message to marijuana users. Citing the Shafer Commission report, he called for reduced penalties for marijuana offenses. "Penalties against drug use should not be more damaging to the individual than the use of the drug itself," he told Congress. "Nowhere is this more clear than in the laws against possession of marijuana in private for personal use." Powerful antidrug organizations—primarily associations of parents—pushed back, and Carter let the issue drop.

The next US president, Republican Ronald Reagan, who took office in 1981, escalated the Drug War once more. By then, drug abuse specialists referred to heroin, cocaine, methamphetamines, and other addictive substances as hard drugs but called marijuana a soft drug—an acknowledgment that it was less dangerous than other drugs. In a radio address to the nation in 1982, Reagan made it clear that he made no distinction between these categories. He stated, "We're making no excuses for drugs—hard or soft, or otherwise. Drugs are bad, and we're going after them. . . . We've taken down the surrender flag and run up the battle flag. And we're going to win the war on drugs."

Like Richard Nixon, Reagan ignored scientific data, including a study from the National Academy of Sciences that found no evidence of harm caused by marijuana use. He dismissed additional studies on the medical benefits of marijuana. Reagan increased the federal budget for drug interdiction (the seizure and destruction of drug shipments coming across US borders) and other antidrug efforts. During Reagan's first term, Congress passed the Comprehensive Crime Control Act of 1984. Among other provisions, this law raised federal penalties for the cultivation, sale, and possession of marijuana. It also authorized local law enforcement agencies to seize property belonging to suspected marijuana dealers, sell it, and use the money to purchase weapons and equipment for police officers on the job.

Reagan's wife, Nancy, joined the antidrug crusade with her Just Say No (to drugs) campaign, aimed at young people. Organizations such as Drug Abuse Resistance Education (DARE) and the Partnership for a Drug-Free

Washington Redskins quarterback Doug Williams presents First Lady Nancy Reagan with a "Just Say No" jersey in 1988. Many celebrities joined Reagan in encouraging children to reject drug use.

America used TV and radio ads and classroom visits to warn children about the dangers of drugs. Many antidrug activists of this era supported Harry Anslinger's gateway theory—the idea that marijuana leads users to more dangerous, more addictive drugs. Carlton Turner, Ronald Reagan's chief drug policy adviser, echoed Anslinger when he said, "No young person starts with cocaine. They start with marijuana, alcohol or pills and go up. Our single best indicator of who's using cocaine is who has used marijuana over 100 times."

BUSTED!

In the last decades of the twentieth century, millions of Americans were using marijuana for both medical and recreational purposes. In doing so, they were breaking federal and state laws. Most marijuana users knew they were breaking the law, but most took pains not to get caught, by smoking discreetly in their own homes, for instance. Those who did get caught found themselves in varying degrees of trouble, depending on where they lived and the exact nature of the crime.

In some states, marijuana laws were lenient. For instance, anyone charged with possessing, transporting, or using less than 1 ounce (28 grams) of marijuana in Colorado faced a maximum fine of only $100. In Oklahoma, on the other hand, marijuana offenders could end up with long prison sentences. Oklahoman Will Foster smoked marijuana to relieve the pain of chronic arthritis and grew cannabis plants in his home. In 1997 he received a ninety-three-year prison sentence: seventy years for marijuana cultivation, twenty years for possessing marijuana in the presence of a child (his daughter), two years for possessing marijuana with intent to distribute it, and one year for failure to pay a state drug tax. Foster was also ordered to pay $62,000 in fines. Oklahoman Jimmy Montgomery, paralyzed from the waist down and confined to a wheelchair, smoked marijuana to boost his appetite and to control severe muscle spasms caused by the spinal injury that had disabled his legs. In 1992 he was sentenced to life in prison for intent to distribute 2 ounces (57 g) of marijuana. Recreational marijuana smoker James Geddes, also from Oklahoma, was sentenced to 150 years in prison for growing five cannabis plants. All three men were eventually released on parole—Foster and Montgomery after a few years in prison and Geddes after eleven years.

In many low-income, inner-city neighborhoods, the police were extremely aggressive about arresting marijuana offenders. In poor neighborhoods of New York City, for instance, starting in the mid-1990s, police used a tactic called stop-and-frisk: they apprehended pedestrians who exhibited "suspicious behavior" (for instance, walking back and forth in front of a store, perhaps in preparation for a robbery) and searched them for weapons, drugs, and other illegal materials. Because the police practiced stop-and-frisk mostly in low-income black and Latino neighborhoods, the majority of those frisked were residents of those neighborhoods—primarily black and Latino, and mainly men. The practice was designed to head off crime before it occurred, although some studies showed it to be ineffective. What it did bring about was the arrest of many people carrying small amounts of marijuana. Police in other cities were similarly aggressive about pursuing marijuana offenders in low-income neighborhoods. But the police didn't use stop-and-frisk or other tough antidrug tactics in more affluent, white neighborhoods, so people there who used marijuana generally did so without getting caught.

CALIFORNIA LEADS THE WAY

Risking arrest, Americans continued to use marijuana as medicine. During the 1980s and 1990s, San Francisco was a hub of gay culture in the United States. Starting in the early 1980s, the city's gay male population was hit hard by the human immunodeficiency virus (HIV), which can develop into acquired immunodeficiency syndrome (AIDS), a deadly disease that can be spread through sex and dirty needles. Many AIDS patients suffered from wasting syndrome, or severe weight loss. They found that smoking or eating marijuana increased their appetites and helped them maintain their weight. Marijuana also helped relieve neuropathic (nerve-based) pain in AIDS patients and relieved nausea and other side effects brought on by powerful pharmaceutical medications used to treat AIDS. In the mid-1980s, a number of AIDS activists in San Francisco organized programs to distribute marijuana to AIDS patients.

California Republican gubernatorial candidate Dennis Peron speaks to supporters in January 1998 at the Rainbow Smoke Shop in San Jose, California. Peron was the author of Proposition 215, which voters approved in 1996 to legalize medical marijuana in California.

Dennis Peron, a resident of San Francisco who had been arrested in the late 1970s for selling marijuana, was arrested again in 1990, this time for providing marijuana to his boyfriend, who was desperately sick with AIDS. After the man died, Peron decided to devote his energy to making medical marijuana available to those who needed it. In 1991 he founded the San Francisco Cannabis Buyers Club. The club provided marijuana to anyone with a doctor's note stating that they had a condition that could be helped by the drug. By the mid-1990s, the club had eleven thousand members, about half of them AIDS patients. Similar buying clubs opened in other big cities in California and in other states with populations hit hard by HIV/AIDS. The clubs operated in violation of state and federal law.

In 1995 Peron and other marijuana activists spearheaded a campaign to make medical marijuana legal in California—despite its prohibition under federal law. The activists used California's ballot proposition process, which allows voters instead of state legislators to make decisions about new laws. Activists got enough signatures to put Proposition (Prop) 215 on the ballot for elections in 1996. The proposition asked voters to decide if medical marijuana should be legalized. Forces for and against the proposition campaigned aggressively. One pro-215 TV advertisement featured Anna Boyce, a sixty-seven-year-old nurse whose husband, J. J. Boyce, had died of cancer. She told viewers, "The nausea from his chemotherapy was so awful it broke my heart. So I broke the law and got him marijuana. It worked. He could eat. He had an extra year of life. Proposition 215 will allow patients like J. J. [to use] marijuana without becoming criminals. Vote yes on 215. God forbid someone you love may need it."

Antilegalization forces included many California law-enforcement officials, district attorneys (whose job is to prosecute criminals), and antidrug organizations. They attacked the proposition on a number of fronts. They pointed out that the proposed law would allow marijuana use for just about any ailment, with only a doctor's recommendation rather than a legal prescription. They predicted that Californians would abuse the system, faking illness to obtain marijuana for recreational use. Anti-215 forces further warned that the law would provide loopholes for drug dealers, allowing them to traffic (sell) recreational marijuana under regulations designed for medical marijuana. Finally, the anti-215 campaign stressed that the proposition sent a dangerous message to kids: that marijuana is a safe and healthy substance, which many argued it was not. General Barry McCaffrey was the nation's "drug czar," serving under then US president Bill Clinton. He was director of the Office of National Drug Control Policy, created in 1988. McCaffrey came to California to campaign against Prop 215. He told voters, "There is not a shred of scientific evidence that shows that smoked marijuana is useful or needed. This is not science. This is not medicine. This is a cruel hoax." He warned that legalizing medical marijuana in California would bring about "increased drug abuse in every category."

On November 5, 1996, voters went to the polls and approved Proposition 215, with 56 percent voting in favor of the law. For the next thirteen years, federal agents routinely raided California marijuana dispensaries, destroyed cannabis plants, and arrested providers and patients. Dispensaries just as routinely reopened their doors. More states, inspired by the California example, began to legalize medical marijuana. Federal agents carried out raids in these states as well—until the federal government announced with the 2009 Ogden memo that it would shift its priorities and put its drug enforcement resources elsewhere.

marijuana as medicine

In 1649 British botanist Nicholas Culpeper published *The Complete Herbal*—a book about the healing powers of plants. He said this about cannabis:

> Boiled in milk, and taken [the seed] helps those that have a
> hot or dry cough. An emulsion [tincture] made from the seed
> is good for [the disease] jaundice, particularly if there be an
> ague [fever] accompanying it. . . . The emulsion or decoction
> [extract] of the seed . . . eases the colic [stomach pain], and
> allays [lessens] the troublesome humours of the bowels. It also
> [stops] bleeding at the mouth, nose and other places. It kills
> worms in man or beast and if the juice is dropped into the ears,
> it will kill worms in them and draw forth earwigs and other living
> creatures. The decoction of the root allays inflammations of the
> head, or any other parts. The herb or distilled water of it does
> the same. A decoction of the root eases gouty pains, hard knots
> in the joints, and pain in the sinews [tendons] and hips. The
> fresh root mixed with a little oil and butter is good for burns.

In the United States of the early 1800s, drugstores made their own medicinal cannabis products and sold them locally. In the late 1800s, pharmaceutical companies such as Parke, Davis & Co. (now Pfizer) and Lloyd Brothers (later bought by a French firm) began to produce brand-name cannabis products such as these. The big firms distributed their medicines nationwide.

Culpeper's assessment of the healing powers of cannabis was based on anecdotes and observations. During his era, scientists had little knowledge about the workings of the human body. But in the following centuries, medical science improved, and soon doctors set out to learn more about the medical benefits of cannabis.

William B. O'Shaughnessy, an Irish doctor, worked at the British-run Medical College of Calcutta in India in the mid-nineteenth century. Noting widespread use of marijuana in India and neighboring countries, he decided to study the plant's medical efficacy. He tested it on patients suffering from rabies, cholera, tetanus, epilepsy, rheumatism, and other illnesses. In a forty-page document published in 1842, O'Shaughnessy called marijuana a "powerful and valuable substance," effective as a painkiller, muscle relaxant, sedative, and stimulant to appetite, and an "anti-convulsive remedy of the greatest value." The British government published a more comprehensive study, the three-thousand-page *Report of the Indian Hemp Drugs Commission,* in 1894. The study concluded that "the occasional use of hemp in moderate doses may be beneficial . . . this use may be regarded as medicinal in character."

In the United States, most studies on marijuana were undertaken later, in the twentieth century, and not to assess its medical benefits but to identify ways in which it might harm human health. For instance, in the late 1930s, New York City mayor Fiorello La Guardia appointed a committee of doctors and scientists to study marijuana, to determine if it was indeed as harmful as Harry Anslinger and other politicians said it was. The committee's report, issued in 1944, concluded that "prolonged use of the drug does not lead to physical, mental, or moral degeneration, nor have we observed any permanent deleterious [harmful] effects from its continued use."

"A MEDICAL TREASURE TROVE"

A turning point in marijuana research came in 1964 in Israel. There, Raphael Mechoulam, a chemist at Hebrew University in Jerusalem, became the first researcher to isolate THC, cannabis's psychoactive ingredient. In the following years, Mechoulam identified additional chemical compounds unique to cannabis. He named the substances cannabinoids and, because of marijuana's long history of use in medicine, predicted that they would prove to be "a medical treasure trove."

Back in the United States, in 1968 the US government opened a cannabis farm at the University of Mississippi in Oxford to grow plants for government-sponsored research on marijuana. Again, this research was primarily undertaken to look for the drug's negative health effects, to back up the government's assertion that marijuana was a dangerous drug.

In one US government–funded study, carried out in the late 1980s, researchers at

> "The [US] government wanted bad things found out about marijuana, and I didn't find them."
>
> —Dr. Tod Mikuriya in the late 1960s, reflecting on his marijuana research with the National Institute of Mental Health, 2004

Saint Louis University School of Medicine in Missouri discovered that the human body and brain have receptor sites that interact with THC and other cannabinoids, creating physical and mental responses. In later US studies, researchers found one kind of receptor (CB1, named for *cannabinoid*) in the brain, in areas responsible for regulating memory, thinking, pain, coordination, movement, appetite, and emotions. They found another kind of receptor (CB2) in the brain and in other organs and body parts, including the digestive system, spleen, liver, heart, kidneys, bones, blood vessels, and reproductive organs. Researchers called this network of receptors the endocannabinoid system, named for the ancient Greek word *endon* (within) and for cannabis. They learned that the endocannabinoid system regulates many biological functions, including body temperature, blood pressure, metabolism, reproduction, memory, pain, hunger, and sleep. The system also naturally produces its own cannabinoids, substances that help keep the body healthy.

JOINTS FROM UNCLE SAM

From 1976 to 1992, the US government itself ran a little-known medical marijuana program, despite the federal ban on the drug. The Compassionate Investigational New Drug program was created in response to a federal lawsuit brought by a man who had been arrested for using marijuana to treat his severe glaucoma, an eye disease. The program supplied about thirty patients with pre-rolled joints made with marijuana from the government's cannabis farm at the University of Mississippi.

In 1992 AIDS patients flooded the program with applications. At that point, President George H. W. Bush, continuing Ronald Reagan's tough stance against drugs, closed the program to new applicants.

Discovery of the endocannabinoid system was key in helping researchers figure out exactly how marijuana affects the brain and body. Marijuana users had long known that ingesting THC causes a number of mental effects, including a slowed reaction time, impaired memory, impaired coordination, altered thinking, euphoria, and reduced pain sensitivity. By studying how TCH and other cannabinoids interact with CB1 and CB2 receptors in the brain and body, researchers could figure out exactly how and why these reactions take place. They could better understand the physical and mental effects—and possible health benefits—of ingesting marijuana.

TRIAL AND ERROR

Mark was forty-five years old, in 2013, when he learned that he had Parkinson's disease, a disorder of the nervous system. Parkinson's kills nerve cells in the brain that release dopamine, a chemical that helps regulate movement and behavior. Mark's first Parkinson's symptoms were a slight tremor in his right arm and muscle aches. He knew that the disease would likely progress and make it more difficult for him to move, balance, and do precise work with his hands. He visited a neurologist in his hometown of Phoenix, Arizona, who prescribed Sinemet, a pharmaceutical drug that would replace the dopamine in Mark's brain. The neurologist told Mark to take the drug as needed to help calm his tremors and ease his pain.

At the same time, Mark also researched medical marijuana. He learned that some Parkinson's patients reported fewer tremors and a greater ease of movement when they used marijuana. Although his neurologist was skeptical, Mark signed on to Arizona's legal medical marijuana program. He began using a low-THC/high-CBD cannabis oil, similar to the type that Charlotte Figi takes to control her epileptic seizures. He ingests the oil using a vaporizer. Similar to an e-cigarette, this device heats the oil, turning it into a gas, which a user can then inhale through a tube. Because the oil contains very little THC, it does not make Mark high. He can "vape" at work with no interference with job performance. Mark also occasionally smokes marijuana that is high in THC. He pays for both the CBD oil and the smokable marijuana out of his own pocket. Health insurance plans in the United States do not pay for a patient's medical marijuana.

Mark uses both marijuana and Sinemet to control his Parkinson's symptoms. He reports that the Sinemet works better than the CBD oil in calming his tremors but that the CBD oil works faster. He notes that the high-THC marijuana is most effective for relieving pain. He also says that the CBD oil gives him more flexibility in treating his tremors. For instance, Sinemet cannot be taken within several hours of eating, whereas Mark can use CBD oil at any time.

Mark's use of marijuana to treat his Parkinson's disease is somewhat informal and experimental. This is because the medical marijuana industry in the United States does not yet fit into US and Western models of medicine. In the Western model, a doctor writes a prescription for a specific drug, at a specific dose, which a patient usually takes according to a prescribed schedule. With medical marijuana, on the other hand, patients like Mark typically experiment to see which doses and which marijuana products work best for them. They take advice from marijuana-friendly medical doctors about how much and what kind of marijuana to use, and they consult with nurse practitioners and customer service staff at marijuana dispensaries. But official, government-issued guidelines on how much and what kind of marijuana to use for what illnesses do not yet exist.

"AT THE MOMENT, IT'S A MESS"

Medical marijuana is not a standardized, uniform product. Patients can ingest it in many forms and by many methods: by smoking it; by vaping; or by eating a variety of baked goods, candies, and other foods made with cannabis-infused butter. Dispensaries also sell marijuana-infused balms and salves to rub on the skin, marijuana tinctures to place under the tongue, CBD oil inside capsules, and other products.

At the New Mexicann dispensary in Santa Fe, New Mexico, patients can buy buds of smokable marijuana from a strain of the cannabis plant called CBD Harlequin. The dispensary recommends the strain for pain, inflammation, muscle spasms, and anxiety. Dispensary sales literature says that the psychoactive cannabinoid THC constitutes 5 percent of CBD Harlequin buds and that the nonpsychoactive cannabinoids CBD and CBG together constitute 10.2 percent. New Mexicann sends all its products to a laboratory for testing to make sure that the advertised cannabinoid levels are accurate, but it also acknowledges that cannabinoid levels can be hard to standardize. In a letter to an alliance of medical marijuana patients, the company explains, "The top bud [of a cannabis plant] . . . might test out at 25% THC, while a lower bud . . . might test out at 20% THC, while a good bud from another side of the plant might test out at 16% THC." The dispensary further explains that cannabinoid levels for a given strain can vary, depending on whether the plant is grown indoors under lights that are fixed in place or outdoors under sunlight that changes through the course of the day. "Bottom line," writes the dispensary, "no two buds on any given plant will test the same." New Mexicann says that its advertised cannabinoid percentages are averages. "What a patient gets in their bag may be more potent but it may also be less," the dispensary concludes.

Other dispensaries face the same problem in trying to standardize doses. In a 2015 study, primarily funded by the Johns Hopkins School of Medicine in Maryland and published in the *Journal of the American Medical Association (JAMA),* researchers tested seventy-five different marijuana edibles sold by dispensaries in California and Washington State. Testing revealed that only 17 percent of the labels listing THC content were accurate. About 60 percent of the products contained less THC than was listed on the label, while 23 percent contained more THC. And as long as labels are not accurate, patients can't rely on medical marijuana for consistency in dosage—which translates into inconsistency in the product's medical benefits. This situation frustrates Raphael Mechoulam,

Medicine Man Denver is a shop in Colorado that sells marijuana for both medical and recreational use. Proper dosage of medical marijuana depends on the person, the illness or condition being treated, and the way the drug is ingested. Patients should always consult with a trusted medical professional before beginning a treatment plan.

the Israeli researcher who first identified THC in the 1960s. He remarks, "People get one thing [dose] today and another thing tomorrow. That's not the way to do medicine. The doctor tells you to take this, in this amount, in such and such a way. Everything people get should be well defined and well analyzed. At the moment, it's a mess. And I'm not happy with it."

In the United States, the Food and Drug Administration (FDA) is in charge of overseeing the safety and effectiveness of most pharmaceutical drugs and medical devices. But the FDA doesn't oversee medical marijuana since the federal government considers marijuana to be harmful instead of medically beneficial. In fact, no central US organization oversees medical marijuana use. Each of the twenty-three states with medical marijuana programs issues its own guidelines for how its program will operate. Each state has different rules about what diseases and conditions qualify a person for medical marijuana. Each state has different rules about dispensary and nursery (growing) operations, how much marijuana a patient can purchase in a given time period, whether patients can grow their own marijuana at home, and how many marijuana plants a patient or marijuana nursery can grow at one time. Many states require dispensaries to ensure that medical marijuana is free of contaminants. For instance, dispensaries in Massachusetts must test products for heavy metals, pesticides, and mold—all of which can make marijuana users sick—but other states don't require the same testing. Compared to the established Western medical industry, the medical marijuana industry is in its infancy. It remains a patchwork of varying state laws and regulations—all of them in conflict with federal law and none of them ensuring consistent, safe products for patients.

A DEARTH OF DATA

Every state with a medical marijuana program requires that a patient have a doctor's written recommendation for medical marijuana use, but not all doctors in those states support medical marijuana. Many doctors aren't convinced that marijuana is useful medicine. Others believe that using marijuana—especially by smoking it—is harmful. The opinions vary because even as hundreds of thousands of people across the nation have signed up for state medical marijuana programs, the science to support medical marijuana has lagged behind. Scientists don't yet know how effective marijuana is in treating a variety of health conditions.

In February 2014, Orrin Devinsky and Daniel Friedman, doctors at the New York University Comprehensive Epilepsy Center, wrote an opinion piece in the *New York Times*. Titled "We Need Proof on Marijuana," the essay discussed epilepsy patient Charlotte Figi and her remarkable success with CBD oil. But the piece also advised caution.

HOW THE FDA DOES IT

Many health professionals would like to see medical marijuana subjected to the same testing procedure used by the Food and Drug Administration to approve pharmaceutical drugs for sale in the United States. This process, called a clinical trial, is designed to discover how new medications work in humans. A principal investigator, often a medical doctor, leads the study, assisted by other doctors, nurses, other health-care professionals, and social workers. The trial involves four phases:

Phase 1 determines whether the treatment is safe. The drug is given to a small number of healthy volunteers to determine its safety, dosage, and side effects.

Phase 2 determines whether the treatment works as intended. The drug is given to a larger group of people to assess if it is both safe and effective for the condition it is intended to treat.

Phase 3 is used to compare the treatment to existing treatments used for the same condition. Thousands of people take the drug at multiple medical centers. This phase of the study confirms the effectiveness of the drug, monitors side effects, and compares the drug with other treatments. Phase 3 studies are random and double-blinded, which means that neither the patient nor the researcher knows who receives the medication and who receives a placebo, or dummy treatment.

Phase 4 examines whether the treatment has other potential uses besides the one under study and whether patients will suffer any long-term adverse effects by using it. This phase may involve millions of people taking the drug for years to identify long-term side effects. During this phase, doctors are legally allowed to use the medication for purposes other than the one for which it was originally intended.

Devinsky and Friedman noted that the effectiveness of CBD oil in treating epilepsy is still only anecdotal, based on the experiences of many patients but not on rigorous scientific evidence. The doctors asked, "Where is the data showing that marijuana is effective for epilepsy?"

One can ask the same question about marijuana and Parkinson's disease. Several studies have shown some promise in treating Parkinson's with marijuana. At the 2013 International Congress of Parkinson's Disease and Movement Disorders in Sydney, Australia, researchers from Israel reported on a study of seventeen Parkinson's patients who used marijuana to control their symptoms. The patients reported decreased tremors, less rigidity in their muscles, and decreased pain. They reported drowsiness as a primary side effect of their cannabis use.

But a handful of studies with small numbers of patients is not nearly enough to tell doctors what they need to know about treating neurological diseases with marijuana. "There is not sufficient evidence to make any definitive conclusions regarding the effectiveness of marijuana-based products for many neurological conditions," wrote the American Academy of Neurology in a position statement in December 2014. Dr. Anup Patel, who authored the statement, explained that studies on marijuana and the treatment of diseases such as epilepsy, multiple sclerosis, and Parkinson's disease were "not as robust as we need them to be." He said that more trials are necessary to evaluate marijuana's effectiveness as a neurological medicine.

Many doctors agree that more trials are needed. But in the United States, any researcher wishing to carry out medical marijuana studies on human subjects comes up against roadblocks. Because marijuana is classed as a Schedule I drug, US scientists who want to study the effects of marijuana on humans must jump through many bureaucratic hoops. They must receive approval for their studies from the DEA and the FDA. They must also apply to the National Institute on Drug Abuse, which runs the government marijuana farm at the University of Mississippi, to obtain a supply of research-grade marijuana. Until June 2015, when the

Research scientist Suman Chandra inspects cannabis plants at the National Center for Natural Products Research at the University of Mississippi in Oxford. The center supplies research-grade marijuana to US scientists who want to study the drug. Before researchers can carry out such studies, however, they must receive approval from several federal agencies.

requirement was dropped, researchers also had to win approval from the US Public Health Service (PHS). In 2011 Sue Sisley, a psychiatrist and then an assistant professor at the University of Arizona, attempted to get the necessary government approvals for a study of whether marijuana was effective in treating military veterans with post-traumatic stress disorder. She encountered a mass of red tape and delays, including nearly three years waiting for approval from the PHS. For studies involving non–Schedule I drugs, the approval process is considerably shorter and easier.

Many nations outside the United States, including Canada, Israel, and many countries in Europe, are more supportive of marijuana research, so a number of studies on human patients have come from these places. At the same time, scientists in the United States have carried out marijuana studies on animals instead of humans and have done research on human cells in the laboratory. But to really understand whether marijuana is effective medicine, US scientists say they need numerous and rigorous studies carried out on human subjects, with federal government approval and federal funding.

To reach this goal, many US doctors have called for the reclassification of marijuana to the Schedule II or Schedule III level, so they can more easily carry out rigorous studies on its efficacy. In June 2014, thirty members of Congress joined the fight for reclassification in a letter addressed to Sylvia Burwell, the US secretary of health and human services. The letter read, "We believe the widespread use of medical marijuana should necessitate research into what specific relief it offers and how it can best be delivered for different people and different conditions. Yet, the scientific research clearly documenting these benefits has often been hampered by federal barriers."

In their 2014 opinion piece, Devinsky and Friedman said that they had received the necessary government approvals and would soon begin a study of the efficacy of using marijuana to treat children with epilepsy. They said that the Schedule I designation "hamstrings doctors from

◇◇

"We believe the widespread use of medical marijuana should necessitate research into what specific relief it offers and how it can best be delivered for different people and different conditions. Yet, the scientific research clearly documenting these benefits has often been hampered by federal barriers."

—US Congress, letter from thirty congressional members to Sylvia Burwell, US secretary of health and human services, 2014

◇◇

performing controlled studies." They continued, "While it is possible to study Schedule 1 drugs in a controlled laboratory setting, it is extremely difficult to study these substances in patients. . . . To foster research, we need to change compounds derived from marijuana from Schedule 1 to a less restrictive category."

KNOWNS AND UNKNOWNS

More than one million Americans are legally using medical marijuana in states where it has been approved. They and the doctors, citizens, and politicians who support state medical marijuana programs believe that marijuana is an effective treatment for certain conditions and symptoms, even without exhaustive studies to back up this assertion.

In his 2014 book *Cannabis Pharmacy,* marijuana policy expert Michael Backes examines twenty-nine health conditions and diseases for which marijuana is being used as a treatment in the United States. The list includes anxiety disorders, appetite disorders, arthritis, attention deficit hyperactivity disorder, autism spectrum disorder, cancer, diabetes, gastrointestinal disorders, glaucoma, hepatitis C, HIV/AIDS, insomnia, migraines, multiple sclerosis, nausea and vomiting, pain, Parkinson's disease, post-traumatic stress disorder, and seizure disorders. Backes's discussions are filled with phrases such as, "inconsistent results," "more research is needed," "anecdotal evidence," "few clinical trials," and "far from proven." These terms reflect that doctors simply don't know how well medical marijuana works for specific conditions.

Still, enough studies have been done to allow researchers to draw some conclusions. For example, in 2015 researchers analyzed seventy-nine studies of medical marijuana, from a variety of different nations, involving sixty-five hundred patients. Their report, published in *JAMA,* stated that marijuana was effective in treating nausea, vomiting, pain, and muscle spasms caused by multiple sclerosis. However, the researchers found little evidence that marijuana was helpful to people suffering from depression, anxiety, sleep disorders, and other ailments for which marijuana is commonly prescribed. Other studies have found marijuana to be effective in treating neuropathic pain and inflammation.

Such studies are a start, but most researchers want to see marijuana put through the thorough trials required by the FDA in the approval of pharmaceutical drugs. Many doctors say that it's premature for states to approve marijuana as a treatment for diseases without that process. "It is unclear why the approval process should be different from that used for other medications," write Drs. Deepak Cyril D'Souza and Mohini Ranganathan in *JAMA*. Raphael Mechoulam agrees, "If you have so many people using [marijuana], there should be clinical evidence."

NO TIME TO WASTE

Despite the doubts and cautions coming from the medical community, many patients—especially those with potentially terminal illnesses such as cancer and AIDS—see no need to wait for more tests. Many gravely ill patients say that medical marijuana helps them cope with the pain, nausea, vomiting, and loss of appetite caused by their diseases or by chemotherapy treatments. Some terminal patients also find that marijuana elevates their mood—relieving some of the emotional distress that accompanies terminal illness.

Cancer patients and AIDS patients were some of the early activists in the fight for legalized medical marijuana in the late twentieth century, and such patients have long defied the law to obtain marijuana to relieve their symptoms. In states where medical marijuana remains illegal, many patients continue to do so. In these states, they often turn to street dealers for marijuana.

Advocates say that both the US medical establishment and the law are behind the curve when it comes to medical marijuana. They regret that many Americans still don't have access to the drug. And even in some states where medical marijuana is legal, marijuana growing and distribution systems are not yet in place. This means that patients have to wait, often for many months, to buy it legally. For example, New York approved a medical marijuana program in summer 2014, but it took more than a year for the state to award licenses to growers and sellers, a delay that frustrated many sick New Yorkers. "Thousands of patients in New York State deal with excruciating pain each day and simply can't wait for the wheels of government to turn," said state assemblyman Brian Kolb. "Bureaucracy should not stand in the way of relief for people suffering from debilitating illnesses and diseases."

for better or worse

Advocates say that the benefits of medical marijuana can be great. They point out that marijuana is usually far safer than pharmaceutical drugs used for the same conditions.

Consider the pharmaceutical drug Humira, used to treat arthritis. The website Drugs.com lists eighteen common side effects resulting from use of Humira and includes this warning:

> Some people using Humira have developed a rare fast-growing type of lymphoma (cancer). This condition affects the liver, spleen, and bone marrow, and it can be fatal. Humira can also lower [levels of] blood cells that help your body fight infections and help your blood to clot. Serious and sometimes fatal infections may occur during treatment with Humira. Call your doctor at once if you have symptoms such as fever, night sweats, weight loss, feeling full after eating only a small amount, pain in your upper stomach, easy bruising or bleeding, dark urine, or jaundice (yellowing of the skin or eyes).

Alternatively, a person suffering from arthritis might choose to use medical marijuana, which for some arthritis patients helps reduce joint inflammation and pain.

Many doctors might argue that marijuana is not as effective as Humira and other pharmaceutical treatments for arthritis. And marijuana is not without side effects either. The most commonly reported side effects, according to Michael Backes, are coughing (caused by smoking marijuana), rapid heartbeat, dry mouth, dizziness or lightheadedness, and red and irritated eyes. Marijuana—especially strains that are high in THC—can also make users feel anxious or panicky.

But none of these side effects is potentially fatal. In fact, no one has ever died of an overdose of marijuana. Research into the endocannabinoid system explains why. The brain stem—the part of the brain that controls breathing and heartbeat—contains very few cannabinoid receptors. So a person who uses excessive amounts of marijuana might feel extreme emotional distress, but because the drug has little effect on the brain stem, the overdose will not stop his or her heart or lungs and lead to death.

Former professional football player Nate Jackson notes that the NFL freely hands out potentially addictive pharmaceutical painkillers to injured players but prohibits the use of safer medical marijuana. His tell-all 2013 memoir, *Slow Getting Up: A Story of NFL Survival from the Bottom of the Pile,* discusses his football injuries and his preferred use of marijuana to reduce the pain caused by those injuries.

Marijuana advocates say that those suffering from severe pain would be better off using marijuana than using the powerful pharmaceutical painkillers that doctors are likely to prescribe. Nate Jackson, who played in the National Football League (NFL) in the first decade of the twenty-first century, says that team doctors freely hand out opiate-based painkillers to injured football players. But such drugs are not necessarily safe. Jackson cites data from the US Centers for Disease Control and Prevention showing that nearly seventeen thousand Americans die from painkiller overdoses each year—and those numbers are on the rise. Prescription painkillers can also be addictive, leading patients who can no longer get the drugs legally to seek out less expensive, illegal, and even more dangerous opiates such as heroin. (The massive surge in US opiate and heroin use has been called an epidemic and made front-page headlines in 2015.) For these reasons, Jackson preferred to use marijuana to treat the pain he endured after suffering broken bones, torn muscles, and separated and dislocated shoulders on the playing field. Although Jackson's decision violated NFL rules, it carried few of the health risks associated with prescription painkillers, of which the NFL approves.

SMOKE SCREENS

Many critics of medical marijuana use point to the dangers of smoking. Scientists have long known that smoking cigarettes causes lung cancer, heart disease, and other serious health problems, so it makes sense to wonder whether smoking marijuana does too. A University of Mississippi study revealed that cannabis smoke contains about fifteen hundred different chemicals. Some of them, including benzene and carbon monoxide, are known to be carcinogenic, or cancer causing. Even so, studies on links between marijuana smoking and cancer have had mixed results. One 2006 study from the University of California–Los Angeles found that regular marijuana smokers who didn't smoke cigarettes were no more likely than anyone else to develop head, neck, or lung cancers. But a 2008 study from the Medical Research Institute

GATEWAY IN REVERSE

Opponents of legalized marijuana frequently cite the gateway theory—the idea that marijuana use leads a person to use harder, more dangerous drugs, such as cocaine and heroin. But numerous studies have shown that the majority of marijuana users do not move on to hard drugs. For instance, the Marijuana Policy Project reports that more than 107 million Americans born since 1960 have tried marijuana. Of that group, 37 million have tried cocaine, and only 4 million have tried heroin. Substance-abuse experts say that most users of hard drugs begin not with marijuana but with nicotine and alcohol. But regardless of what drugs someone tries first, experts dispute the claim that the use of any one drug necessarily leads to the use of another.

New research suggests that marijuana might actually be a sort of reverse gateway—a vehicle for helping people give up more dangerous drugs. A 2014 University of Pennsylvania study found that in states where medical marijuana was legal, death rates from opiate (opium-based painkiller) overdoses were on average about 25 percent lower than in states without medical marijuana. The study also found that the drop in overdose deaths was greater in states where medical marijuana had been available longer. These data suggest that many patients with severe pain have switched from opiates to safer and legal medical marijuana, leading to a reduction in opiate overdose deaths.

of New Zealand found that long-term, heavy marijuana smokers (who also didn't smoke cigarettes) were six times more likely to get lung cancer than those who didn't smoke marijuana. The New Zealand researchers noted that cannabis smokers tend to inhale more deeply than cigarette smokers and hold smoke in their lungs longer—in an effort to get a greater high. For heavy marijuana users, this practice might make smoking marijuana even more dangerous than smoking tobacco. However, other studies show that occasional marijuana users are no more likely to get lung cancer than anyone else.

The jury is still out on whether marijuana smoking causes lung cancer, but researchers do say that marijuana smoking can lead to respiratory irritation and illnesses such as bronchitis. To protect their airways and lungs, many medical marijuana patients choose alternatives to smoking. They use vaporizers or ingest edible marijuana products, including marijuana-infused cookies, candies, and even kale chips.

Vaping delivers cannabinoids to the bloodstream just as quickly as smoking does—in five to ten minutes—whereas the effects of edible marijuana can take between thirty and ninety minutes to kick in. The effects of edible marijuana can also last twice as long as those of smoked or vaped marijuana. Because of these time differences, patients who choose edible marijuana over smoked or vaped marijuana must be careful. Patients have reported eating medical marijuana cookies, for instance, and then finding themselves—more than an hour later—filled with anxiety or panic, because they've accidentally taken in too much THC. They can then only wait until the effects of the drug wear off, and that can take several more hours. With smoked or vaped marijuana, on the

IS VAPING SAFE?

Medical marijuana advocates often steer patients to vaporizing. It is considered healthier for the respiratory system than smoking marijuana. Some patients use small, portable vape pens, which are similar to e-cigarettes. But like e-cigarettes, these devices are new to the market and haven't been thoroughly tested by the FDA.

Some scientists warn that the chemicals found inside some vape pens, particularly propylene glycol, might be toxic or carcinogenic when heated and inhaled. Project CBD, an organization that studies the medical benefits of CBD and other cannabinoids, wants to see more rigorous testing and regulation of vape pens and other vaporizers to protect patient safety.

other hand, a patient can inhale from a pipe or vaporizer and then quickly evaluate (within ten minutes) whether the medicine is doing its job—relieving pain, calming tremors, or relieving nausea, for example. If not, the patient can inhale again to ingest more medicine. So patients who smoke or vape have more control over their marijuana dosages than those who use edible marijuana.

DR. FEEL GOOD

Many critics say that it's too easy to get a prescription for medical marijuana in states where the drug is legal. For example, in Oregon 93 percent of patients enrolled in the state's medical marijuana program report "severe pain" as their qualifying condition. Some suspect that many of these patients are fakers, exaggerating or making up pain symptoms to get doctors to sign the forms required for access to affordable marijuana. (Recreational marijuana is also legal in Oregon and available at stores across the state. But because of tax laws, it's much more expensive to buy recreational marijuana than the medical marijuana sold at dispensaries.)

California has the least strict medical marijuana laws in the nation. The state places no limits on how much marijuana a patient can buy at one time. Patients can grow their own marijuana at home—again with no limits. The list of medical conditions that qualify someone to use medical marijuana includes those commonly found on other state lists, including cancer, HIV/AIDS, epilepsy, and multiple sclerosis. But the list also includes "any debilitating illness where the medical use of marijuana has been 'deemed appropriate and has been recommended by a physician.'" This means that just about anyone with a health complaint can use medical marijuana, as long as a physician signs off on it.

Critics say that California's rules are far too lax—and that they make it too easy for people who want to use marijuana recreationally to qualify as medical marijuana patients. Critics also charge that unscrupulous California doctors are raking in easy money by making questionable medical marijuana recommendations. In *Men's Health* magazine, journalist Cassie Shortsleeve elaborates, "In California, a mental health condition—such as depression or anxiety—can score you a medical marijuana card. Walk up and down Venice Beach [a Los Angeles neighborhood] and you'll see doctor-office storefronts boasting 24-hour live patient verification. If you have some cash, an ID, and a qualifying medical condition, you're well on your way to weed [marijuana]."

Writer Jacob Sullum describes "the widespread impression that a large portion of California's medical marijuana patients are using phony or exaggerated ailments as an excuse to get high." But some respond to this charge: So what? Why shouldn't someone who's occasionally ill, depressed, or anxious use marijuana to feel better? In the *Journal of Psychoactive Drugs,* sociologist Craig Reinarman and his colleagues note that "Prozac and other . . . antidepressants . . . are often prescribed for patients who do not meet [American Psychiatric Association] criteria for clinical depression but who simply feel better when taking it." Sullum adds, "If some people find

Rules for the legal purchase of medical marijuana vary by state. At some medical offices in California, people can walk in without an appointment, visit with a doctor, and receive a recommendation for marijuana on the spot. Other states, such as Minnesota, have very strict rules governing access to legal medical marijuana. In these states, it is much more difficult for residents to qualify for and purchase the drug.

that marijuana works better for these purposes, there is no rational reason to prevent them from using it."

Investigative journalist Martin Lee says that marijuana often makes people feel better—whether they are depressed, sick, or not—and that this effect is reason enough to recommend it. "Marijuana makes people laugh, and laughter is therapeutic," he says. He references studies showing that "laughter is excellent medicine for reducing stress [and] boosting the immune system. . . . A good belly laugh can exercise the heart more efficiently than a physical workout. Laughter can even help type-2 diabetics process sugar better."

DR. FEEL BAD

Other experts advise caution. "To claim that cannabis is completely safe and can cause no harm is as irrational as claiming that cannabis has no medical use whatsoever," writes Michael Backes. Yes, people have used cannabis as medicine for thousands of years, he points out, but "humans have used various traditional medicines incorrectly, and have inadvertently harmed [themselves] in the process." Although most side effects of marijuana seem to be minor and short-term, some serious effects have been noted. For instance, marijuana can raise a user's blood pressure, so the drug might be harmful to patients with existing high blood pressure, heart disease, and other heart problems. Backes also says that excessive marijuana use can increase the chances of heart attack and stroke. Studies show that the babies of women who smoke marijuana during pregnancy weigh less than those of women who do not use the drug. The danger here is that children with low birth weights might suffer more health problems as they grow than children of normal weights. Other studies have shown that children whose mothers use marijuana in pregnancy lag behind their peers mentally. Doctors advise breastfeeding mothers not to use marijuana, since the drug can be passed along to their babies in breast milk. Experts point out that marijuana use may also decrease, increase, or interfere with the effects of certain prescribed pharmaceutical drugs.

BIG PHARMA

Pharmaceutical companies are studying marijuana, analyzing its ingredients and using some of these ingredients to make commercial medicines. Most of this work has taken place outside the United States. Journalist Martin Lee says, "After the brain's THC receptor was discovered, Big Pharma [giant pharmaceutical corporations] saw dollar signs and drug-company labs got the green light to explore ways to pharmaceuticalize the ancient herb."

In the early 1980s, for example, a Belgian company called Solvay Pharmaceuticals developed dronabinol, a synthetic (laboratory-made) form of THC. Even though the US government claims that marijuana is not effective or safe medicine, the FDA approved dronabinol to help control nausea and vomiting in cancer patients and weight loss in AIDS patients in 1985. In the United States, the drug is sold in pill form under the brand name Marinol.

Sativex (*pictured below*), created by GW Pharmaceuticals in Great Britain, is a marijuana-based liquid, designed to be squirted under the tongue or inside the cheek. Unlike synthetic Marinol, Sativex is made from the cannabis plant. It contains roughly equal parts THC and CBD. Approved for use in Canada, New Zealand, and many European nations, Sativex is prescribed for cancer pain, neuropathic pain, and muscle spasms caused by multiple sclerosis. GW Pharmaceuticals is seeking FDA approval so that the drug can be sold in the United States. The company is also running trials on Epidiolex, a CBD-based drug for treating epilepsy.

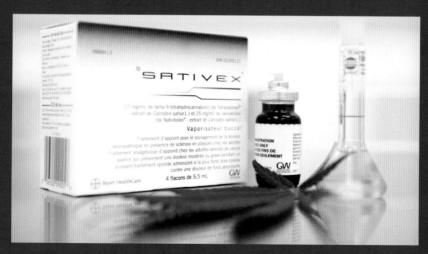

All drugs—even those sold over the counter—come with warning labels, and marijuana is no different. The website drugs.com provides the following warnings to medical marijuana users:

- Do not drive, operate machinery, or perform other hazardous activities while using cannabis. It may cause dizziness, drowsiness, and impaired judgment.
- Do not drink alcohol while using cannabis. Alcohol will increase dizziness, drowsiness, and impaired judgment.
- Cannabis may increase the effects of other drugs that cause drowsiness, including antidepressants, alcohol, antihistamines, sedatives . . . pain relievers, anxiety medicines, seizure medicines, and muscle relaxants.

Research shows that marijuana does indeed impair judgment. It also impairs attention, coordination, reaction time, and motor skills. So it is not surprising that driving under the influence of marijuana is against the law in all states. United Patients Group, a medical marijuana advocacy organization in California, advises patients: "Even if you have a Medical Marijuana Card . . . or doctor's recommendation for marijuana, that valid use of medical marijuana does not protect you from prosecution of a DUI [driving under the influence]. Best bet, be safe and just don't drive after recent use."

BAD FOR BUSINESS

The legalization of medical marijuana in various states has caused a number of conflicts—both with federal laws and with workplace regulations. For example, medical marijuana is legal in Colorado, but the Colorado-based satellite television provider Dish Network is a drug-free workplace. It randomly screens employees for the use of illegal drugs, and when it did so in 2010, employee Brandon Coats tested positive for marijuana. As a result, the company fired him from his job as a customer service rep.

Coats was paralyzed in a car crash at the age of sixteen, and he uses marijuana—in accordance with Colorado law—to control muscle spasms caused by his injury. "It wasn't like I was getting high on the job," Coats said. "I would smoke right before I go to bed, and that little bit would help me get through my days." Regardless, Dish Network does not want marijuana users on its staff, and courts have upheld the rights of businesses to fire or refuse to hire people who fail drug tests, based on the argument that certain drugs compromise worker performance. Companies say that drug-free workplaces create a safer work environment and also lower their insurance costs. And companies that do business

Coloradan Brandon Coats, who is paralyzed from the neck down, uses marijuana to control his severe muscle spasms. Although the use of medical marijuana is legal in Colorado, Coats was fired from his job at Dish Network for violating the company's antidrug policies.

with the federal government must follow federal drug-free workplace laws, regardless of state laws. Coats took his case to court, and in June 2015, the Colorado Supreme Court ruled in favor of Dish Network.

Other conflicts have occurred in facilities that provide hospice care (for the terminally ill), in nursing homes, and in hospitals. Many of these health-care providers receive federal funding, so marijuana use is prohibited there. Afraid to run afoul of federal law and to risk losing this funding, many such facilities prohibit medical marijuana use by residents and patients. This situation angers a Denver man named Caleb, who suffers from Parkinson's disease and terminal rectal cancer. He is enrolled in a hospice-care program, which used to provide him with free medical marijuana but which stopped doing so for fear of breaking federal law. Caleb notes that the facility, which receives some of its funding from federal Medicaid and Medicare programs, can still provide him with powerful legal—and potentially addictive—pharmaceutical drugs, including morphine and Valium. Caleb says that these substances haven't been effective in relieving his cancer and Parkinson's symptoms. He laments, "Those are your tax dollars at work, man. You're paying for the government to spend money [via Medicaid and Medicare] on that box of . . . [pharmaceutical] drugs that I'm not going to touch. That's a waste. But what I really need [marijuana], they can't give me. Does that make sense?"

5

r&r

Many people use marijuana not for medical reasons but because they enjoy the euphoric feeling the drug can provide. For many, marijuana simply provides a way to relax. In 2012, before Washington State approved legalization of recreational marijuana, Seattle-based travel writer and TV personality Rick Steves spoke at a marijuana legalization event in Spokane, Washington. He argued that adults should not be prohibited from using a mind-altering substance in their own homes. "I'm a hardworking, churchgoing, child-raising taxpaying citizen," he told the crowd. "If I want to go home and smoke a joint and stare at the fireplace for two hours, that's my civil liberty."

Many Americans enjoy alcoholic drinks for the same reasons. They use them to relax and also enjoy alcohol's mind-altering properties. Unlike marijuana, alcohol is readily available to all Americans aged twenty-one and older. As long as people don't drink and drive, they are free to consume all the alcohol they want. But data show that alcohol, which is legal in the United States, is much more dangerous than marijuana, which is illegal. According to the CDC, excessive alcohol use leads to approximately eighty-eight thousand deaths each year in the United States. This figure includes deaths from diseases caused by

Advocates for legalized marijuana say that the drug is much safer than alcohol, a product that is widely available to Americans aged twenty-one and older. Alcoholism and alcohol-related deaths are major public health concerns in the United States.

long-term alcohol use—such as liver diseases—and deaths caused by alcohol-related motor vehicle crashes, alcohol poisoning, and alcohol-fueled violence.

Tobacco, another legal substance for Americans twenty-one and older, is even more dangerous. The carcinogens (cancer-causing compounds) and other chemicals that cigarette smokers inhale are known to cause cancer, heart disease, stroke, lung disease, diabetes, and other serious health problems. The CDC says that cigarette smoking is responsible for more than 480,000 US deaths each year. Marijuana is far less deadly. No one has ever taken a fatal overdose of marijuana, and marijuana is not known to cause deadly diseases. But the drug is not entirely harmless either. For example, researchers from Columbia University studied approximately 24,000 US traffic deaths in 2010 and concluded that marijuana use had contributed to 12 percent of them.

QUITTING TIME

Scientists say that over time, heavy marijuana users will build up a tolerance to the drug. That is, it will take more and more marijuana to make them feel high. But whether people can become addicted to marijuana is debatable. The Office of National Drug Control Policy states that one in nine marijuana users will become addicted. But many drug abuse experts say that *addiction* is too strong a word in the context of marijuana use. They reserve the term for much more powerful drugs that create serious physical dependency and often lead to excruciating symptoms when a user goes through withdrawal. For instance, withdrawing from opiate-based painkillers can take weeks or months, and patients might experience nausea, diarrhea, sleeplessness, extreme anxiety, hallucinations, delirium, sweating, confusion, pain, and even seizures during the process. By contrast, someone who gives up marijuana after long-term use "might feel grumpy or have low energy or be somewhat depressed; he or she might not sleep well," writes Martin Lee. However, such symptoms are not physically punishing, and they usually last less than two weeks.

Marijuana advocates acknowledge that users can become psychologically dependent on the drug, but they don't agree that the drug causes full-blown addiction. They also reject the idea that heavy marijuana users need to attend drug rehab programs. True, every year, thousands of people do enter such programs. But between 60 and 70 percent of them do so to fulfill a court requirement after an arrest for a marijuana offense (often with the choice of entering rehab or going to jail). Others are sent to rehab by an employer or a school. Less than 15 percent enroll in rehab voluntarily. The takeaway for advocates is that marijuana is not addictive and that people who really want to quit can successfully do so on their own.

Advocates for marijuana legalization say that tolerating the use of some dangerous substances while punishing the use of a safer substance makes no sense. In an opinion piece in the *New York Times,* journalist Philip M. Boffey acknowledges that marijuana is not completely safe. He writes, "The potency of current strains may shock those who haven't tried it for decades, particularly when ingested as food. It can produce a serious dependency, and constant use would interfere with job and school performance. It needs to be kept out of the hands of minors." But he goes on to stress that "on balance [marijuana's] downsides are not reasons to impose criminal penalties on its possession, particularly not in a society that permits nicotine use and celebrates drinking."

MODERN-DAY PROHIBITION

Most historians agree that Prohibition of the 1920s and early 1930s was a failed experiment. It did not keep Americans from drinking. Nor did it rid the United States of social ills. During Prohibition, ordinary, otherwise law-abiding Americans continued to consume alcohol—but they did so in secret. They could no longer openly sit down at the local saloon for a glass of beer or buy a bottle of whiskey from the neighborhood liquor store. They drank at secret nightclubs, which were frequently raided by the police, and they bought "bathtub gin" and other homemade liquor—much of it of poor quality and some of it poisonous. Criminals such as Al Capone controlled the liquor trade. They made millions of dollars from this underground business and paid no taxes to the government.

Many say that the twenty-first-century prohibition on marijuana is no different. Ordinary, otherwise law-abiding people still use marijuana—but in much of the nation, they do so secretly. They buy the drug on the black market, which is dominated by criminal drug cartels, mostly based in Mexico but also operating in parts of the United States. Except in states with legalized recreational marijuana, medical marijuana, or both, the marijuana supply is unregulated. No agency checks to see that marijuana products are free of mold or other contaminants. No sellers are licensed. And all the money from marijuana sales in states without legalization goes to the black market, since illegal drug dealers do not file income tax returns.

Twenty-first-century marijuana prohibition has created additional social complexities and—many would say—additional injustices. According to the Drug Policy Alliance (DPA), an organization that lobbies for the reform of US drug laws, 700,993 Americans were arrested for violating marijuana laws in

2014. Of this group, 88 percent were arrested for merely possessing marijuana. Journalist Jesse Wegman notes that in 2011, US police made more arrests for marijuana possession than for all violent crimes combined. He wrote in July 2014, "Police departments that presumably have far more important things to do waste an enormous amount of taxpayer money chasing a drug that two states [at the time the piece was written] have already legalized and that a majority of Americans believe should be legal everywhere." According to the American Civil Liberties Union, a group whose mission is to defend individuals' constitutionally guaranteed rights, the United States spends between $1.2 billion and $6 billion per year on enforcing laws against marijuana possession.

Across the nation, many cities and states have reduced penalties for marijuana possession for first-time offenders. Instead of arrest and prison time, offenders receive fines or probation. Many are court-ordered to take part in substance-abuse rehabilitation programs.

◇◇

"I hate to see a great deal of law enforcement resources spent on things like the possession and use of marijuana when we have murder cases, armed robbery cases . . . that go unsolved."

—Vermont US senator Patrick Leahy, 2013

◇◇

But even though some offenders are treated leniently, others can still end up with long prison sentences. For instance, in October 2011, truck driver Bernard Noble of New Orleans, Louisiana, received a thirteen-plus-year sentence for possessing a small amount of marijuana—enough to roll two joints. And a marijuana conviction can haunt an offender for years. Long after any jail time, fines, or other punishments are settled, a marijuana offender might be denied a professional license, a driver's license, insurance, a home or car loan, student financial aid, or access to public housing, depending on state law, the severity of the offense, and other circumstances. Some offenders are permanently barred from voting.

Because of racial profiling, black Americans and other people of color are far more likely than white Americans to be victims of stop-and-frisk and similar law enforcement practices. Blacks and people of color are also much more likely than whites to be arrested for marijuana crimes. Abby Haglage writes in the *Daily Beast,* "Despite data that they use drugs at the same rate as whites, African Americans are 3.73 times more likely to be arrested for marijuana related crimes." According to the Drug Policy Alliance, Latinos are twice as likely as whites to be arrested for marijuana crimes, even though they use marijuana less than both whites and blacks.

In 2014 President Barack Obama discussed this disparity in a *New Yorker* interview: "Middle-class kids don't get locked up for smoking pot, and poor kids do. And African-American kids and Latino kids are more likely to be poor and less likely to have the resources and support to avoid unduly harsh penalties."

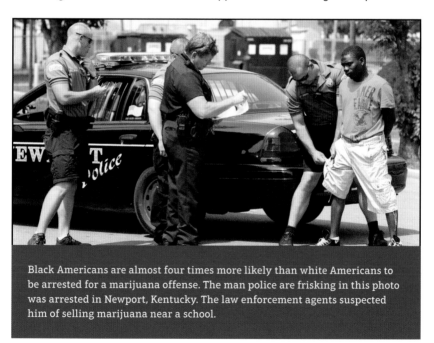

Black Americans are almost four times more likely than white Americans to be arrested for a marijuana offense. The man police are frisking in this photo was arrested in Newport, Kentucky. The law enforcement agents suspected him of selling marijuana near a school.

He added, "We should not be locking up kids or individual users for long stretches of jail time when some of the folks who are writing those laws have probably done the same thing [used marijuana]. . . . It's important for society not to have a situation in which a large portion of people have at one time or another broken the law and only a select few get punished."

LEGALIZE IT!

Advocates for legalization say that ending the prohibition on marijuana and creating a taxed and regulated marijuana industry would be a win-win-win for the United States. First, the federal and state governments could tax marijuana sales, bringing large amounts of new revenue into government coffers. Second, a legal marijuana industry would provide competition to criminal cartels and other black market dealers. They might not be put out of business completely, but their profits would be reduced if they had to compete for business with honest marijuana sellers. Finally, a legalized marijuana industry would allow law enforcement and the courts to use more of their resources to apprehend and prosecute violent criminals instead of small-time marijuana offenders. This shift in priorities would also help relieve prison overcrowding.

Colorado and Washington State have seen these predictions fall into place. A report by the Economic and Revenue Forecast Council, for example, shows that Washington State is projected to take in $694 million from taxes on the state's marijuana industry by the middle of 2019. That money will be shared among health-care, education, and substance-abuse-prevention programs, as well as other state projects. In Colorado marijuana is expected to bring in $134 million in taxes for the fiscal year beginning in July 2015. Most of that money will go toward substance-abuse treatment efforts, programs designed to keep children and teenagers from using marijuana, public health efforts, and law enforcement programs.

Legal marijuana sales do seem to be undercutting the black market. Because of medical and recreational legalization, the US marijuana industry is booming. Cannabis plants are being grown in high-tech greenhouses and are being bred for specific THC, CBD, and other cannabinoid content. Daniel

Vinkovetsky, who writes for *High Times* magazine, says that the US product is superior to that grown in Mexico, where most black market marijuana originates. He explains, "Mexican marijuana is considered to be of poor quality generally because it's grown in bulk, outdoors; it's typically dried but not really cured [more carefully dried to enhance flavor and remove harshness], which is something we do here in the U.S. with [high-quality] cannabis." A Mexican cannabis farmer in the state of Sinaloa says that his business is on the decline. "Two or three years ago, a kilogram [2.2 pounds] of marijuana was worth $60 to $90. But now they're paying us $30 to $40 a kilo. . . . If the U.S. continues to legalize pot, they'll run us into the ground."

Of course, the cartels that control the Mexican marijuana trade won't just close up shop and go away in the face of US competition. Mexican journalist Javier Valdez says, "I believe that now, because of the changes they're having to make because of marijuana legalization in the U.S., the [Sinaloa] cartel is pushing more cocaine, meth, and heroin. They're diversifying." This assessment shows that marijuana legalization, while it may eliminate some problems associated with the illegal drug trade, will not solve all of them.

With the legalization of marijuana, advocates also predict fewer arrests and fewer marijuana offenders clogging courts. In Colorado this transformation is stark. According to a 2015 report from the Drug Policy Alliance, Colorado has seen a 90 percent drop in marijuana possession charges since 2010, as well as a 96 percent drop in cultivation charges and a 99 percent drop in distribution charges. "It's heartening to see that tens of thousands of otherwise law-abiding Coloradans have been spared the [absurdity] of getting handcuffed or being charged for small amounts of marijuana," said Art Way of the Colorado chapter of the DPA. The Colorado Center on Law and Policy estimates that the state saved between $12 million and $40 million in marijuana-related law enforcement costs in the first year of legalization alone.

proceed with caution

Police officers in La Follette, Tennessee, are no strangers to contraband (smuggled) marijuana. Many times, they have pulled over vehicles for speeding or other traffic violations and found packages of dried marijuana buds hidden inside trunks and beneath seats. With its pungent scent, even when it's not being smoked, smokable marijuana is hard to keep secret. In spring 2015, officers in La Follette pulled over a Chevy Blazer and seized a very different kind of marijuana contraband: containers full of marijuana cookies, gingerbread-man-shaped marijuana candies, marijuana marshmallows, and a tub of marijuana butter.

Marijuana edibles have become wildly popular in the United States. In states where marijuana is legal, customers can buy them premade and packaged in retail shops. In states such as Tennessee, where marijuana is illegal, the snacks are more likely to be made at home using cannabis butter. Many marijuana users prefer eating marijuana to smoking it, but the marijuana-in-food trend has given cause for alarm. First, marijuana is more potent, slow-acting, and long-lasting when eaten than when smoked or vaped. The drug can sneak up on you. That is, you might eat a high-THC marijuana cookie and find yourself unpleasantly agitated an hour or more later. Usually, the anxiety and panic will pass in a few hours. But in extreme

Sweet Grass Kitchen, a gourmet bakery in Denver, sells marijuana-infused edibles such as these cookies.

cases, people who overdose on THC might suffer from hallucinations and other mental disturbances.

A tragic example comes from Denver. There, Wyoming college student Levy Thamba, visiting the city with his friends for the specific purpose of buying marijuana legally, ate a marijuana cookie from the Native Roots Apothecary in early 2014. The lemon poppy-seed cookie contained 65 milligrams (0.002 ounces) of THC. The label on the package said that one cookie contained 6.5 servings (enough TCH to get more than six people high), and the store clerk told Thamba and his friends to "cut the cookie into six pieces and to only eat one piece [each]." Thamba didn't follow this advice. At a hotel room where he and his friends were staying that night, he ate the entire cookie—ingesting more than six times the recommended amount of THC. He fell asleep and then woke up in a state of great anxiety.

FAKE AND POSSIBLY FATAL

While marijuana itself has never been shown to be fatal, a product frequently billed as synthetic marijuana can be a killer. Known on the street by various names, including spike, spice, or K2, this illegal drug is made of synthetic cannabinoids sprayed onto dried and shredded plant material. When smoked or vaped, it provides a quick high, not unlike that achieved with real marijuana. But spike can also cause seizures, swings in heart rate and blood pressure, kidney failure, respiratory failure, anxiety, confusion, hallucinations, and violent behavior. Some people have died after ingesting the drug. It is illegal in the United States, but some gas stations, drug paraphernalia shops, and Internet businesses have been caught selling it.

Marijuana advocates, drug abuse specialists, and doctors are quick to point out that synthetic cannabinoids behave differently in the brain and body than do the natural cannabinoids found in marijuana. Says emergency room doctor and toxicologist (poison specialist) Jeff Lapoint, "This is *not* marijuana. It should not be thought of like marijuana. We have to get this out there: Its effects are serious. It's a totally different drug."

As the morning wore on, his behavior became more and more disturbed. He began talking to a lamp in the hotel room. He smashed furniture, lamps, and a television set and then ran from the room and fell over a balcony railing, plummeting four floors to his death. In another horrific incident, a Denver man ate marijuana-infused candy and a few hours later began ranting and raving. He then took out a gun and killed his wife. This and the Thamba case are rare examples of marijuana-induced psychosis (mental illness involving loss of touch with reality), but public health officials worry that more cases are on the horizon.

Dr. Mahmoud ElSohly, who runs the US government's marijuana research program at the University of Mississippi, explained in 2013, "There are more emergency room admissions today than ever because of marijuana use. That's simply because of the psychoactive side effects of the high THC content that the public uses." Consider that in 1998 the average marijuana plant contained about 4.5 percent THC. By 2015 the average in Colorado was above 18 percent. And customers who want marijuana with even more THC can buy it. One marijuana shop in Boulder, Colorado, for example, sells hashish with a 70 percent THC level.

THE CHILDREN'S HOUR

Despite debates about whether marijuana should be legalized, almost everyone agrees that children and teenagers should not use the drug recreationally (and most agree that only severely ill children, such as those with epilepsy or a terminal illness, should use the drug medically). Levy Thamba was nineteen years old when he died. He was too young to legally purchase marijuana in Colorado. A friend had bought the cookie for him. Although underage, Thamba was old enough to know that marijuana is a mind-altering drug. But many younger children have no way of knowing that certain cookies and other sweets—some of them designed to look like gummy bears, lollipops, and Jolly Rancher candies—actually contain marijuana.

Colorado law requires marijuana shops to sell edibles in child-resistant packaging and to clearly label ingredients, THC content, and serving sizes. And in theory, children should never be marijuana consumers anyway—since the law forbids sales to those under the age of twenty-one. But some children are getting hold of marijuana edibles brought home by their parents. Between January and October 2014, fourteen children were brought to the emergency room at Children's Hospital in Denver, after unknowingly eating marijuana. None were seriously harmed.

Colorado officials became so concerned about marijuana overdoses and accidental ingestion by children that in 2014 the state's Department of Public Health and Environment suggested banning all edible marijuana sales. That proposal was eventually pulled, but the state did set new limits on how much THC any single marijuana snack can legally contain. Advocates for edible marijuana say that it's up to parents to keep the drug away from their children—just as it's up to parents to keep liquor and other harmful substances from kids. Lindsay Topping, marketing director for Denver's Dixie Elixirs and Edibles, which sells marijuana-infused drinks and candies, stresses, "I can't control how a parent stores this. It's out of my hands once it gets into that home."

DAZED AND CONFUSED

Studies show that in the short term (over a twenty-four-hour period) marijuana use can disrupt focus, memory, decision making, and motivation—which can interfere with school and job performance. And studies have demonstrated that teenage marijuana users perform less well in school than nonusers. A 2013 University of Maryland study found that even infrequent marijuana users are more likely to drop out of college than nonusers. In one study published in the *Journal of Neuroscience*, researchers scanned the brains of forty college-age adults, half of whom had been smoking marijuana for more than a year and half of whom did not use the drug. In the smokers, the scans revealed "abnormalities in

BLOW OUT

Many marijuana users prize a highly potent substance called hash oil, also known by the nicknames earwax and shatter. This oil, containing highly concentrated THC (in some cases as much as 90 percent), can be smoked, vaped, or used in place of butter in preparing marijuana edibles. Medical marijuana advocates recommend it for those suffering from severe pain, whereas recreational users like it for its extreme high.

One popular method for extracting hash oil from marijuana involves using butane. Butane is highly flammable, and even a tiny spark can cause it to explode. In Colorado butane extraction was responsible for thirty-two explosions in homes and marijuana processing facilities in 2014. Explosions have occurred in other states as well. The mishaps have sent dozens of people to the hospital with severe burns and other injuries.

the shape, density and volume of the nucleus accumbens," a region of the brain involved with motivation, pleasure, pain, and decision making. That marijuana affects the brain is not surprising or new, but experts say that our brains continue to develop into our mid-twenties and that heavy marijuana use by young people can interfere with this development.

Much marijuana research has been controversial. For example, a 2012 Duke University study claimed to find a link between marijuana use and the decline in IQ (intelligence quotient) among teenagers. But follow-up studies found no such link and also criticized the original study's methodology. Other research suggests that marijuana use might encourage the development of schizophrenia (a severe mental disease characterized by delusional thinking) in certain young people. A later study from Harvard Medical School found fault with this research as well. When faced with such contradictory studies, advocates for and against legalized marijuana tend to cite the research that fits their agenda and to criticize the research supporting the opposite argument.

Marijuana supporters say that education, not prohibition, is the key to keeping kids away from drugs. But opponents of legalized marijuana say that prohibition can play an important role—because most kids don't want to break the law. When asked by the Partnership for Drug-Free Kids why they do not use marijuana, young people commonly answer that they do not want to get in trouble with the law and do not want to disappoint their parents. But if marijuana is legal for parents, opponents say, kids will get the message that the drug is acceptable and will be more likely to use it.

About 44 percent of US teenagers say that they have tried marijuana at least once. About 21 percent of high school seniors report using marijuana in the past thirty days. And despite the best efforts of states to convince children not to use marijuana—such as a Colorado campaign funded by marijuana taxes—the drug seems to be gaining further acceptance among teens. Every year, a project called Monitoring the Future, run by the University of Michigan and funded by the National Institute on Drug Abuse, surveys young people regarding their attitudes about drug use.

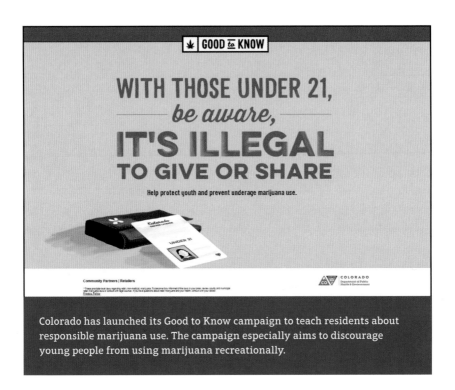

GOOD to KNOW

WITH THOSE UNDER 21,
be aware,
IT'S ILLEGAL
TO GIVE OR SHARE

Help protect youth and prevent underage marijuana use.

Community Partners | Retailers

COLORADO
Department of Public
Health & Environment

Colorado has launched its Good to Know campaign to teach residents about responsible marijuana use. The campaign especially aims to discourage young people from using marijuana recreationally.

In the 2009 survey, 52.4 percent of high school seniors said that they believed marijuana smoking to be harmful. By 2014 that figure had dropped to 36.1 percent.

Experts note that as long as kids are still using marijuana, the black market will survive and thrive—since even in states where marijuana use is permitted, a person has to be at least twenty-one to buy the drug legally. At the University of Colorado in Boulder, a twenty-two-year-old named Zach earns extra cash by legally buying medical marijuana from a dispensary and reselling it to students who are too young to make legal recreational purchases. Even those who are old enough to make legal purchases often choose instead to buy from Zach, because by law, recreational shops must charge sky-high city and state sales taxes. Zach's medical product, taxed at one-third the rate, can be bought and resold much less expensively. For opponents of legalized marijuana, such transactions poke holes in the "legalization will kill off the black market" argument. The story also supports claims that legalization makes it easier for young people to obtain marijuana.

ON THE ROAD

The United States already has significant problems with drug and alcohol abuse. According to Mothers Against Drunk Driving, twenty-eight Americans die in drunk driving crashes every day. Opponents of legalized marijuana say that such problems will only get worse if we add more legal marijuana to the mix. One 2012 study, published in the *British Medical Journal,* showed that those who drive within three hours of smoking marijuana are twice as likely to be in a car crash that leads to serious injury or death than drivers who are sober. By contrast, in 2015 the US National Highway Traffic Safety Administration issued a report saying that drivers who test positive for marijuana are no more likely to crash their cars than those who are sober.

The term *test positive* holds the clue to the widely different conclusions of the two reports. People can test positive for marijuana long after they are no longer impaired by the drug, because traces of THC remain in the bloodstream for days or even weeks after marijuana use. In Colorado the police arrest drivers whose THC-to-blood measurement exceeds a certain level. But the blood test doesn't provide reliable information about whether someone is actually fit to drive because THC remains in the bloodstream for such a long time. This imprecision in testing has led to some drugged-driving arrests for marijuana users who were sober. That might soon be changing, as several companies are developing marijuana breathalyzers that will provide a more accurate assessment of whether a driver is impaired.

Many marijuana opponents say that legalization has made roads and highways in the United States less safe. According to the Colorado State Patrol, in the first half of 2014, 12.5 percent of citations issued for impaired driving in the state were given to drivers who were under the influence of marijuana.

In Washington State, a traffic safety commission found that the number of THC-influenced drivers involved in fatal car crashes jumped 48 percent between 2013 and 2014.

THE STONED AGE

Like medical marijuana users, recreational users can be legally fired from their jobs if they fail an employer-administered drug test, even if they are not impaired at work. Critics say that the laws need to change—to accommodate the legal use of marijuana and to reflect the peculiarities of THC remaining for so long in the bloodstream. But marijuana legalization is in its infancy and it could take several years before the law catches up with what's happening on the ground.

In Colorado and the other states where recreational marijuana use is legal, some businesses are tolerant of employees who use the drug on the job. However, the vast majority of employers want workers to be sharp, alert, and clearheaded—and that means no marijuana use at work. Even many marijuana businesses prohibit on-the-job use. After all, their employees are selling a potent drug and handling large amounts

"I think, by any measure, the experience of Colorado has not been a good one unless you're in the marijuana business. We've seen lives damaged. We've seen deaths directly attributed to marijuana legalization. We've seen marijuana slipping through Colorado's borders. We've seen marijuana getting into the hands of kids."

—Kevin A. Sabet, executive director of the organization Smart Approaches to Marijuana, 2014

The popularity of e-cigarettes has exploded. However, public health officials, law enforcement officers, and parents note that some young people are using the devices to secretly ingest marijuana.

of cash. They must not lose focus. "Just as we wouldn't want folks going out and having a two- to three-martini lunch, we shouldn't have folks going out and smoking a joint during lunch," said David Kochman, an attorney representing Open Vape, a Denver-based company that sells marijuana vaporizers.

Regardless of laws and regulations, it is difficult to control who uses marijuana and when. For instance, in Washington State, thousands of people vape cannabis oil with e-cigarette-style devices called e-joints. State law prohibits marijuana use in public, but vapers have found that they can take discreet hits from e-joints, and no one seems the wiser. "In this day and age, everybody has a vapor pen," said Shy Sadis, who vapes at Seattle Seahawks football games and elsewhere. "You don't know if they're smoking marijuana or nicotine." The e-cigarette trend has

"Let me tell you, there is nothing more inconsistent with trying to improve mental health and reduce substance-abuse disorders in this country than to legalize [another] drug."

—Patrick Kennedy,
former US representative of Rhode Island, 2014

caused alarm among public health officials, who worry that the devices are hooking kids on nicotine, an extremely addictive drug, and perhaps leading them to use even more dangerous smoked cigarettes. Officials are equally concerned about e-joints, which appear to be giving kids even easier access to marijuana. Barbara Carreno, a spokeswoman for the DEA, explains, "If you go on Instagram, you will find hundreds of thousands of postings by kids on how they are using variants of e-cigarettes, or e-cigarettes themselves, to smoke pot in the presence of their parents and at school, and getting by [undetected]."

THE GENIE IN THE BOTTLE

Many say that far from being a remedy for the problems that resulted from the Drug War, the legalization of marijuana has simply created new problems—and more problems. Many Americans are organizing to fight further legalization or to repeal it where it has already passed. An organization called Arizonans for Responsible Drug Policy is an example. In a press release of March 30, 2015, Seth Leibsohn, the organization's chairperson, presents an argument for halting legalization. He wrote,

> Just about 20 years ago or so, drug dealers were seen for what they were—criminal and dangerous elements in our society

that were shunned by the mainstream and those who cared about our children's health. People who dealt and sold marijuana were seen as losers, or worse. . . .

What was once scorned is now hyped and celebrated. . . .

Today, marijuana dealers have been mainstreamed . . . they now run state-sanctioned dispensaries. . . .

With the mainstreaming of that which was once considered dangerous and marginalized, we are unleashing a dangerous experiment on society, with a drug that is becoming more and more dangerous through its increased potency. . . .

Now is not the time to further legitimize such a dangerous substance by making it more and more available. No—the toxic [element] should be marginalized once again, and that includes those who want to peddle and profit from it. . . . Let's put the genie back in the bottle right now, before it affects more people, or indeed, an entire generation, that we will one day have to apologize to if we further unleash today's marijuana on them.

the ganjapreneurs

The marijuana business is booming. After voters legalized recreational marijuana in Oregon in 2014, the state handed out about thirteen hundred business licenses to new marijuana retail shops, nurseries, processors, and wholesalers. All these businesses will create jobs for budtenders (marijuana salespeople) and other employees in the legal marijuana industry. In Colorado retail marijuana sales (medical and recreational combined) totaled nearly $700 million in 2014. The ArcView Group, a marijuana-based investment firm, notes that legal marijuana accounted for $2.4 billion in sales in the United States in that same year. That was a 74 percent jump over 2013. *Marijuana Business Daily,* an online magazine, estimated that the marijuana industry put about $10 billion into US state and local economies in 2015. And the numbers are projected to keep rising.

Across the nation, people see dollar signs when they look at marijuana. So-called ganjapreneurs (named for *ganja,* a Hindi word for "cannabis," and *entrepreneurs*) are rushing into the industry in droves. Many new businesses provide services to the marijuana industry. For instance, one company wants to open a credit union—a type of bank—to serve only marijuana businesses. Some firms sell software designed specifically for

Legalization of marijuana has led to many new enterprises. For example, chef Dani Fontaine (*third from left*) leads a Denver cooking class. She teaches students how to make marijuana-infused foods.

medical marijuana dispensaries. Other businesses specialize in marijuana packaging, processing, and growing equipment.

Many ganjapreneurs focus on the marijuana consumer. HelloMD, based in San Francisco, electronically connects medical marijuana patients with doctors. Patient and doctor speak Skype-style via computer, to determine whether the patient is eligible for a recommendation for medical marijuana. Other businesses sell vaporizers, provide marijuana delivery services, offer marijuana cooking classes, or run dating websites to match up marijuana users with romantic partners.

Marijuana on its own is a big seller. One company is developing marijuana-infused pork jerky, sausage, and smoked salmon. In April 2015, country singer Willie Nelson announced that he would launch his own brand of marijuana, Willie's Reserve, to be sold in states where the product is legal.

"When I see images of people . . . who are now trying to run legitimate marijuana businesses, they're almost all white. . . . After 40 years of impoverished black men getting prison time for selling weed, white men are planning to get rich doing the same things."

—Michelle Alexander, **author of** *The New Jim Crow: Mass Incarceration in the Age of Colorblindness,* **2014**

In Denver, visitors can stay at marijuana B&Bs (bed and breakfasts), which provide marijuana along with food and accommodations. The *Cannabist* is a slick online magazine, sponsored by the *Denver Post,* devoted to the latest political, cultural, and scientific news about marijuana. Jake Browne is the *Cannabist*'s marijuana critic. His job is to sample the different strains of marijuana sold at city businesses and to rate them for flavor, potency, and psychoactive effect.

The explosion in marijuana business has some people worried. They say that Big Pharma has already entered the marijuana industry, with Marinol long established on the market and other products in development. Industry watchers believe that Big Tobacco is gearing up to produce marijuana cigarettes in the event of nationwide legalization. Commentators say that if and when big corporations enter the marijuana industry, they might quickly crush the competition. Then the little start-ups and mom-and-pop companies that have dominated the industry in its early years will go out of business.

NOT SO FAST

Despite brisk sales, it's not easy to run a marijuana business. Under federal law, marijuana is illegal, which leads many banks to refuse to do business with marijuana shops and dispensaries. Regardless of state law, bankers worry about running afoul of federal law enforcement and federal bank regulators. According to the US Treasury Department, of the more than 100,000 banks and credit unions operating in the United States, only about 105 will work with marijuana businesses.

The result for many marijuana shops is literally a flood of cash. Businesses without banking services cannot accept checks or credit cards, which have to pass through a bank for processing. All customers must therefore pay in cash, and the businesses must pay their vendors, employees—and even tax collectors—in cash. Some marijuana businesses move large amounts of money in armored cars, hire armed guards, and store cash in heavy safes. All this cash makes the businesses much more vulnerable to robbery than businesses that have access to banking services.

Marijuana businesses have also encountered a web of confusing and restrictive tax laws. Some of these businesses have faced massive tax bills resulting from a 1982 federal law designed to fight drug trafficking. NORML and other marijuana advocacy groups are lobbying in Washington, DC, to reform banking and tax laws so that legal marijuana businesses can operate competitively and efficiently like other legal businesses. These efforts include the Marijuana Businesses Access to Banking Act, introduced into the US Senate in July 2015. The bill (and a similar one introduced earlier into the US House of Representatives) has been referred to a congressional committee for further discussion. Political insiders think that its passage is unlikely as long as marijuana remains prohibited under federal law. To improve their chances of success with legislative action, many marijuana businesses make donations to political candidates who support marijuana legalization and the reform of restrictive federal laws and regulations.

CRITICAL MASS

In 1979 CBS News began polling Americans about whether they supported the legalization of marijuana for recreational use. The first poll revealed that less than one-third of Americans—27 percent—did so. In polls since then, the number favoring legalization has climbed steadily. In April 2015, the same CBS News poll found 53 percent of Americans in favor of legalization.

GLOBAL TRENDS

As in the United States, marijuana laws are changing around the world, with more countries considering legalizing the drug for medical use, recreational use, or both. Medical marijuana is legal in some countries, including Austria, Canada, the Czech Republic, Finland, Germany, Israel, Italy, the Netherlands, Portugal, and Spain. The most liberal recreational laws are found in Portugal, which decriminalized all drug use in 2001, and Uruguay, where marijuana can be purchased legally from government outlets. A few other nations, including Colombia, Spain, and Switzerland, allow people to grow and possess small amounts of marijuana for personal use.

As in the United States, where state-by-state legalization continues, the global lists are in flux, as various nations reconsider and change their marijuana regulations. In Canada, Justin Trudeau, elected prime minister in October 2015, announced that he would spearhead a campaign to legalize recreational marijuana in his nation. Other countries considering legalization include Jamaica, Mexico, and Spain.

A Gallup poll in October 2015 put the number at 58 percent. The CBS poll also revealed that 43 percent of Americans have tried marijuana, up from 34 percent in a 1997 poll, and 84 percent support the use of marijuana for medical purposes.

As support for marijuana grows, the nation is likely to see more states approving the drug for medical as well as recreational use. In early 2015, campaigns to legalize recreational use were building momentum in Ohio, Nevada, California, Massachusetts, and Arizona. Of that group, the first state to vote on the issue was Ohio. There, in November 2015, citizens rejected a plan to legalize both medical and recreational marijuana—in part because the proposal would have put control of the state's marijuana industry in the hands of only ten powerful businesses.

Despite the loss in Ohio, legalization forces are on the move. The *Washington Post* reports that eleven states might vote on recreational legalization in 2016 and five other states might put medical marijuana on the ballot.

Some people compare the US marijuana legalization movement to the push to legalize gay marriage. In the first decade of the twenty-first century, same-sex marriage was legal in only a handful of US states and was illegal under federal law. But pro—gay marriage forces kept fighting, and by early 2015, gay marriage was legal in thirty-seven states. In June 2015, the US Supreme Court ruled that all states must recognize same-sex marriages. Marijuana legalization might be heading in the same direction. As more and more states legalize the drug, the legalization movement will build critical mass—perhaps enough to carry the entire nation to legalization. Catherine Hiller, author of *Just Say Yes: A Marijuana Memoir,* elaborates: "It's hard for people to change their mind-set after so many years. But look at marriage equality [gay marriage] and how that happened so fast. That was unheard of five years ago. So maybe smoking pot will be completely normal, and no one will raise an eyebrow when they find out somebody smokes."

WHAT WILL THE FEDS DO?

Medical marijuana has many supporters in the US Congress. In December 2014, Congress passed the Rohrabacher-Farr Medical Marijuana Amendment, which prohibits the US Justice Department from spending any money to interfere with state medical marijuana programs, although the provision was effective only through 2015. In March 2015, three senators introduced the Compassionate Access, Research Expansion, and Respect States Act (Senate Bill 683), which would permanently prevent federal intervention in state marijuana programs, move marijuana from Schedule I to Schedule II, and also allow Veterans Administration physicians to prescribe medical marijuana to veterans of the US military. The bill was referred to a Senate committee. If the bill passes, it will dramatically transform the US medical marijuana industry, especially in the area of research.

HOPE FOR HEMP

Hemp—or cannabis with less than 0.3 percent THC—was once a common and profitable crop in the United States. It was used to make textiles, food, paper, and other products. But when the US government outlawed marijuana in the mid-twentieth century, it also outlawed hemp cultivation (although hemp products could be imported from other nations). That prohibition ended in 2014. That year's US Farm Bill authorized states to conduct research and begin to pilot agricultural programs to restart the US hemp industry. Many states have already begun this work.

The reborn hemp industry might help solve environmental problems. For instance, to whiten paper made from wood, papermakers use large amounts of toxic chemicals. Hemp is lighter in color than wood, so hemp paper can be whitened using fewer and safer chemicals. Hemp can also be grown with fewer pesticides and herbicides than other textile crops, such as cotton, because it has a built-in resistance to bugs and weeds. Furthermore, hemp can be used as a biofuel—a fuel made from plant material. Biofuels release fewer climate-changing gases into the atmosphere than the fossil fuels coal, oil, and natural gas. Some builders have started working with a substance called hempcrete, which is made by mixing the woody interior of hemp stalks with water and lime. Hempcrete is used as nontoxic, airtight insulation (a substance that restricts the loss of heat) in building walls. The newly revived hemp business could be a big moneymaker for the United States. In Canada, hemp is a billion-dollar-a-year industry.

A few groups are wary about the new hemp industry. For instance, the National Narcotic Officers' Associations Coalition says that you can't tell by looking at a cannabis plant whether it contains more or less than 0.3 percent THC. The coalition fears that the legalization of hemp might enable marijuana growers to fool the authorities by hiding behind the facade of legal hemp cultivation. Despite this concern, hemp has many supporters in the US government, including Republican senator Rand Paul, who believes that hemp farming could help bring jobs and prosperity to his home state of Kentucky.

For many decades, marijuana was illegal and US farmers were not allowed to grow hemp (cannabis with low THC levels). New laws have opened the door to a revived US hemp industry. Builders can now use hemp (*below*), esparto grass, and other fibers in light concrete, plasterboard, and other common construction materials.

But while the federal government seems to be growing more supportive of medical marijuana, recreational use still has many opponents at the highest levels of government. That became clear in July 2014, when the *New York Times* editorial board called for nationwide legalization with an opinion piece called "Repeal Prohibition, Again." The US Office of National Drug Control Policy responded forcefully a day later. It noted "a cascade of public health problems associated with the increased availability of marijuana." It listed the following arguments:

- Marijuana use affects the developing brain.
- Substance use in school-age children has a detrimental effect on their academic achievement.
- Marijuana is addictive.
- Drugged driving is a threat to our roadways.

The response made it clear that the federal government had no intention of backing nationwide legalization, even though it continued to take a hands-off approach with states that had approved recreational marijuana use. Reinforcing this stance, in 2015 both US attorney general Loretta Lynch and US drug czar Michael Botticelli stated their opposition to federal legalization of marijuana.

But the federal government is always in flux. Different administrations can set the government on a new course—either for or against marijuana legalization. Some Democrats have called for moving marijuana from Schedule I to Schedule II. At the other extreme, some Republicans have called for the recreational marijuana industry to be shut down. If a presidential administration cracks down on either medical or recreational marijuana, a lot of people could be in a lot of trouble—since all marijuana use is still against federal law.

Which way will the pendulum swing on marijuana legalization? No one knows. Those in the pro-marijuana camp are optimistic. Vivian McPeak, founder of Seattle Hempfest, the world's largest pro-marijuana gathering, provides this prediction: "No political or human rights movement in America has made it this far without eventually winning. It's just a matter of time."

Pat Dalrymple, a banker and a newspaper columnist in Colorado, is less certain. He writes, "Advocates of the marijuana industry and the people in it will tell you that the swell of approval of the drug is becoming a tsunami. . . . They argue that there's now no turning back to the dark days of Reefer-phobia. . . . They may very well be right. But what if they're not?" Dalrymple warns that if a presidential administration trades "tacit approval" of marijuana for "explicit enforcement," that means that the federal government could choose to shut down marijuana businesses and even confiscate their assets.

◇◇◇

"Small business owners, medical marijuana patients, and others who follow state laws still live with the fear that a new administration—or this one—could reverse course [on legalization] and turn them into criminals."

—Jared Polis, US representative from Colorado, 2015

◇◇◇

In the end, he cautions, "the feds speak louder than the state." As long as the federal government continues to criminalize marijuana, the United States will continue to have a patchwork of state marijuana laws—and marijuana users and sellers will continue to stand on shaky legal ground.

Source Notes

5   Emma Innes, "We Feed Our Daughter Cannabis to Stop Her Thousands of Seizures Each Week," *Daily Mail.com,* August 13, 2013, http://www.dailymail.co.uk/health /article-2391207/We-feed-daughter-CANNABIS-stop-having-thousands-seizures-week -Parents-say-toddler-say-walk-talk-time-thanks-treatment.html.

5   Ibid.

6   Ibid.

6   Saundra Young, "Marijuana Stops Child's Severe Seizures," *CNN,* August 7, 2013, http:// www.cnn.com/2013/08/07/health/charlotte-child-medical-marijuana/.

7   "Drug Schedules," DEA, accessed February 8, 2016, http://www.dea.gov/druginfo /ds.shtml.

8   Dave Philipps, "Bid to Expand Medical Marijuana Business Faces Federal Hurdles," *New York Times,* August 23, 2014, http://www.nytimes.com/2014/08/24/us/bid-to-expand -medical-marijuana-business-faces-federal-hurdles.html.

10 "Memorandum for Selected United States Attorneys on Investigations and Prosecutions in States Authorizing the Medical Use of Marijuana," DOJ, October 19, 2009, http://www .justice.gov/opa/blog/memorandum-selected-united-state-attorneys-investigations -and-prosecutions-states.

11 Alyson Martin and Nushin Rashidian, *A New Leaf: The End of Cannabis Prohibition* (New York: New Press, 2014), 201.

13 Martin Booth, *Cannabis: A History* (New York: Picador, 2003), 161.

15 Martin A. Lee, *Smoke Signals: A Social History of Marijuana—Medical, Recreational, and Scientific* (New York: Scribner, 2012), 5.

16 Ibid., 17.

17 Booth, *Cannabis,* 86.

20 Lee, *Smoke Signals,* 42.

20 Amanda Reiman, "75 Years of Racial Control: Happy Birthday Marijuana Prohibition," *Huffington Post,* September 28, 2012, http://www.huffingtonpost.com/amanda-reiman /marijuana-prohibition-anniversary_b_1923370.html.

20 Lee, *Smoke Signals,* 52.

22 Brad Rodu, "Gateway Claims Aimed at E-Cigarettes: Counterfeit, Déjà Vu," Heartland Institute, October 29, 2014, http://news.heartland.org/editorial/2014/10/29/gateway -claims-aimed-e-cigarettes-counterfeit-deja-vu.

24 Lee, *Smoke Signals,* 95.

25 Ibid., 121.

25 Ibid., 122.

25 Ibid., 122–123.

25 "DEA History," DEA, accessed May 24, 2015, http://www.dea.gov/about/history.shtml.

26 Lee, *Smoke Signals,* 153.

26 National Commission on Marihuana and Drug Abuse, "Marijuana: A Signal of Misunderstanding," Drub Library, accessed May 24, 2015, http://druglibrary.eu/library /reports/nc/mis2_3.htm.

27 Ibid., 158.

28 Jim Spencer, "First Pot, Then the Hard Stuff," *Chicago Tribune,* August 13, 1985, http://articles.chicagotribune.com/1985-08-13/features/8502220796_1_ tetrahydrocannabinol-marijuana-gateway-theory.

29 Mike Bostock and Ford Fessenden, "'Stop-and-Frisk Is All but Gone from New York," *New York Times,* September 19, 2014, http://www.nytimes.com/interactive/2014/09/19 /nyregion/stop-and-frisk-is-all-but-gone-from-new-york.html.

31 Carey Goldberg, "Medical Marijuana Use Winning Backing," *New York Times*, October 30, 1996, http://www.nytimes.com/1996/10/30/us/medical-marijuana-use-winning -backing.html.

31 Lee, *Smoke Signals,* 246.

31 Ibid.

32 Booth, *Cannabis*, 71.

33 Lee, *Smoke Signals,* 24.

33 Ibid., 24–25.

33 Michael Backes, *Cannabis Pharmacy: The Practical Guide to Medical Marijuana* (New York: Black Dog & Leventhal, 2014), 15.

34 Lee, *Smoke Signals,* 61.

34 Ibid., 82.

34 Ibid., 125.

38 "Answers to the Survey from New Mexico Licensed Non-Profit Producers," Cannagramma, accessed May 27, 2015, http://cannagramma.com/wp-content /uploads/2015/03/SurveyResultsOrig.pdf.

39 David Casarett, *Stoned: A Doctor's Case for Medical Marijuana* (New York: Current, 2015), 237.

42 Orrin Devinsky and Daniel Friedman, "We Need Proof on Marijuana," *New York Times,* February 12, 2014, http://www.nytimes.com/2014/02/13/opinion/we-need-proof-on -marijuana.html.

42 Dennis Thompson, "Medical Marijuana's Use for Brain Disorders," *WebMD*, December 17, 2014, http://www.webmd.com/brain/news/20141217/neurologists-say-jury-still-out-on -medical-marijuanas-use-for-brain-disorders.

42 Ibid.

44 "Thirty Members of Congress Support Eased Medical Marijuana Research," *NBC News*, June 17, 2014, http://www.nbcnews.com/science/science-news/thirty-members -congress-support-eased-medical-marijuana-research-n133321.

45 Devinsky and Friedman, "We Need Proof."

45 Backes, *Cannabis Pharmacy*, 186–193.

46 James Joiner, "Medical Pot Is Bunk and So's You're Brownie," *Daily Beast,* June 23, 2015, http://www.thedailybeast.com/articles/2015/06/23/medical-pot-is-bunk-so-s-your -brownie.html.

46 Casarett, *Stoned*, 237.

47 Johnny Green, "Legislation Introduced to Expedite Access to Medical Marijuana in New York," *WeedBlog*, April 28, 2015, http://www.theweedblog.com/legislation-introduced -to-expedite-access-to-medical-marijuana-in-new-york/.

48 "Humira," *Drugs.com*, accessed May 27, 2015, http://www.drugs.com/humira.html.

53 Aaron Carroll, "Is There Anything Actually 'Medical' about Medical Marijuana," *New York Times*, July 20, 2015.

53 "California Medical Marijuana Law," NORML, accessed May 27, 2015, http://norml.org /legal/item/california-medical-marijuana.

54 Cassie Shortsleeve, "The Truth about Medical Marijuana," *Men's Health,* April 20, 2013, http://www.menshealth.com/medical-marijuana.

54 Jacob Sullum, "How Many Medical Marijuana Patients Are Fakers? Does It Matter?" *Reason.com*, August 5, 2011, http://reason.com/blog/2011/08/05/how-many-medical -marijuana-pat.

54 Ibid.

55 Ibid.

55 Lee, *Smoke Signals,* 173.

55 Backes, *Cannabis Pharmacy,* 26.

55 Ibid.

56 Lee, *Smoke Signals,* 358.

57 "Cannabis," *Drugs.com*, accessed May 27, 2015, http://www.drugs.com/illicit/cannabis .html.

57 "What Is a Marijuana DUI?," United Patients Group, accessed May 27, 2015, http://www .unitedpatientsgroup.com/blog/2012/03/21/what-is-a-marijuana-dui/.

58 Jack Healy, "Legal Use of Marijuana Clashes with Job Rules," *New York Times,* September 7, 2014, http://www.nytimes.com/2014/09/08/us/legal-use-of-marijuana -clashes-with-workplace-drug-testing.html.

59 Casarett, *Stoned*, 4–5.

60 Jonathan Martin, "Marijuana Initiative 502 a Tough Sell in Eastern Washington," *Seattle Times,* last modified October 24, 2012, http://www.seattletimes.com/seattle-news /marijuana-initiative-502-a-tough-sell-in-eastern-washington/.

62 Lee, *Smoke Signals,* 387.

63 Philip M. Boffey, "What Science Says about Marijuana," *New York Times*, July 30, 2014, http://www.nytimes.com/2014/07/31/opinion/what-science-says-about-marijuana .html.

64 Jesse Wegman, "The Injustice of Marijuana Arrests," *New York Times,* July 28, 2014, http://www.nytimes.com/2014/07/29/opinion/high-time-the-injustice-of-marijuana -arrests.html.

64 Martin and Rashidian, *A New Leaf*, 216.

65 Abby Haglage, "Life in Prison for Selling $20 of Weed," *Daily Beast,* February 27, 2015, http://www.thedailybeast.com/articles/2015/02/27/fate-vincent-winslow-got-life-in -prison-for-20-worth-of-weed.html.

66 David Remnick, "Going the Distance," *New Yorker,* January 27, 2014, http://www .newyorker.com/magazine/2014/01/27/going-the-distance-2.

67 John Burnett, "Legal Pot in the U.S. May Be Undercutting Mexican Marijuana," *National Public Radio*, last modified December 2, 2014, http://www.npr.org/sections /parallels/2014/12/01/367802425/legal-pot-in-the-u-s-may-be-undercutting-mexican -marijuana.

67 Ibid.

67 Ibid.

67 "New Report Documents Huge Drop in Colorado Marijuana Arrests since Legalization," *Sentencing Law and Policy* (blog), March 26, 2015, http://sentencing.typepad.com /sentencing_law_and_policy/2015/03/new-report-documents-huge-drop-in-colorado -marijuana-arrests-since-legalization.html.

69 Kieran Nicholson, "Man Who Plunged from Denver Balcony Ate 6x Recommended Amount of Pot Cookie," *Denver Post*, April 17, 2014, http://www.denverpost.com/news /ci_25585976/man-who-plunged-from-denver-balcony-ate-6.

70 Alice G. Walton, "Why Synthetic Marijuana Is More Toxic to the Brain Than Pot," *Forbes,* August 28, 2014, http://www.forbes.com/sites/alicegwalton/2014/08/28/6-reasons -synthetic-marijuana-spice-k2-is-so-toxic-to-the-brain/.

71 Shortsleeve, "Truth about Medical Marijuana."

72 Jack Healy, "New Scrutiny on Sweets with Ascent of Marijuana in Colorado," *New York Times*, October 29, 2014, http://www.nytimes.com/2014/10/30/us/new-scrutiny-on -sweets-with-ascent-of-marijuana-in-colorado.html.

73 Abigail Sullivan Moore, "This Is Your Brain on Drugs," *New York Times*, October 29, 2014, http://www.nytimes.com/2014/11/02/education/edlife/this-is-your-brain-on-drugs-marijuana-adults-teens.html.

76 Jack Healy, "After 5 Months of Sales, Colorado Sees the Downside of a Legal High," *New York Times,* May 31, 2014, http://www.nytimes.com/2014/06/01/us/after-5-months-of-sales-colorado-sees-the-downside-of-a-legal-high.html.

77 Healy, "Legal Use of Marijuana."

77 Kira Peikoff, "No Smoke, but Haze around E-Joint," *New York Times*, January 12, 2015, http://www.nytimes.com/2015/01/13/health/with-the-e-joint-the-smoke-clears-.html.

78 Lee Fang, "The Real Reason Pot Is Still Illegal," *Nation,* July 2, 2014, http://www.thenation.com/article/180493/anti-pot-lobbys-big-bankroll.

79 Seth Leibsohn, "Time to Stop the Credibility of the Marijuana Drug Legalizers," Arizonans for Responsible Drug Policy, March 30, 2015, http://www.arizonansforresponsibledrugpolicy.org/press-releases-2/2015/3/30/44v8ymvpxnp8qy3481iwznxll7rl6i.

82 Michelle Alexander, in Saki Knafo, "White Men Getting Rich from Legal Weed Won't Help Those Harmed Most by Drug War," *Huffpost*, last modified March 7, 2014, http://www.huffingtonpost.com/2014/03/06/michelle-alexander-drug-war_n_4913901.html.

85 David Gonzalez, "Smoking Marijuana for 50 Years and Turning Out Just Fine," *New York Times,* April 12, 2015, http://www.nytimes.com/2015/04/13/nyregion/after-50-years-of-smoking-marijuana-her-life-turned-out-nicely.html.

88 Office of National Drug Control Policy, "Response to the New York Times Editorial Board's Call for Federal Marijuana Legalization," Whitehouse.gov, July 28, 2015, https://www.whitehouse.gov/blog/2014/07/28/response-new-york-times-editorial-marijuana-legalization.

89 Lee, *Smoke Signals,* 393.

89 Pat Dalrymple, "Banking Columnist: Lenders Have Reason to Be Leery of Pot Businesses," *Glenwood Springs Post Independent,* March 15, 2015, http://www.postindependent.com/news/15100970-113/lenders-have-reason-to-be-leery-of-pot-businesses.

89 "US Congress: Legislation Introduced to Get the Feds out of the Marijuana Enforcement Business," NORML, February 26, 2015, http://norml.org/news/2015/02/26/us-congress-legislation-introduced-to-get-the-feds-out-of-the-marijuana-enforcement-business.

Glossary

addiction: the compulsive need for and use of a habit-forming substance. People with an addiction typically develop an increased tolerance for the substance (they must use larger and larger amounts to feel the substance's effects), and they endure specific, often painful and distressing physical symptoms when they stop using it.

black market: the sale and distribution of goods or money in violation of laws and regulations set by a government. Many US marijuana transactions take place on the black market, with no government oversight and with no taxation.

cannabidiol (CBD): a nonpsychoactive cannabinoid found in the cannabis plant. Some studies have shown CBD to be effective in the treatment of certain medical conditions, including epilepsy.

cannabinoids: various chemicals found naturally in cannabis or marijuana. Tetrahydrocannabinol is a psychoactive cannabinoid, while CBD and other cannabinoids are nonpsychoactive.

cannabis: also called hemp; a flowering plant that has been used throughout human history. The stalks of the cannabis plant can be made into rope, cloth, and paper. Cannabis seeds contain a useful oil and can also be eaten. Cannabis leaves and flowers provide the intoxicating drug marijuana.

cartel: a group composed of independent businesses that have joined forces to limit competition or to fix prices. In the context of the drug trade, the term *cartel* refers to a large criminal drug-trafficking organization.

contraband: illegal or prohibited goods

dispensary: a place where medicine or medical treatment is provided

endocannabinoid system: a network of receptors in the human body that interact with cannabinoids and that also help regulate many physiological functions, such as body temperature, blood pressure, metabolism, reproduction, memory, pain, hunger, and sleep

ganjapreneurs: people who have launched or invested in marijuana businesses, especially in the wake of the legalization of recreational marijuana in several states. The name is a combination of the words *ganja* (Hindi for "cannabis") and *entrepreneur* (someone who launches and runs a new business).

gateway theory: the argument, first put forth in the 1950s, that using marijuana leads people to use more dangerous drugs. Numerous studies have disproven the gateway theory.

hashish: resin found in the flowers of female cannabis plants. Hashish can be smoked or eaten for intoxicating effect.

hemp: fibers from the stalks of the cannabis plant, used to make rope, paper, and fabric. The term *hemp* is also a name for the cannabis plant itself.

marijuana: an intoxicating drug made from the dried leaves and flowers of the cannabis plant

opiate: a drug containing or derived from opium, which is a milky substance from the unripened seeds of the poppy plant. Opiates include heroin and morphine. Many synthetic drugs used legally as painkillers have the same chemical makeup as opiates. Used irresponsibly, opiates can lead to addiction and lethal overdose.

pharmaceutical: a medicine developed, processed, and sold by a drug company and usually available only with a doctor's prescription

Prohibition: the era in US history, between 1920 and 1933, when it was illegal to manufacture, sell, or transport alcoholic beverages. The term *prohibition* can also refer to the banning of any substance (such as marijuana) or activity (such as marijuana use).

psychoactive: affecting the mind or behavior. This term is used to describe drugs with an intoxicating, euphoric, or mind-altering effect.

psychosis: derangement of the mind, characterized by delusions, hallucinations, and disorganized speech or behavior

stop-and-frisk: a police practice that involves stopping a person who shows suspicious behavior. Stop-and-frisk is used to prevent crime before it occurs and is often directed disproportionately at people of color. Officers don't need a search warrant to practice stop-and-frisk.

tetrahydrocannabinol (THC): the psychoactive cannabinoid found in marijuana

vaporizer: a device used to heat marijuana or CBD oil, turning it into a vapor, which is then inhaled

Western medicine: the type of medicine most commonly practiced in the United States and other industrialized nations. Western practitioners use pharmaceutical drugs, surgery, advanced diagnostic tests, and other techniques to treat illness and disease.

Selected Bibliography

Backes, Michael. *Cannabis Pharmacy: The Practical Guide to Medical Marijuana.* New York: Black Dog and Leventhal, 2014.

Booth, Martin. *Cannabis: A History.* New York: Picador, 2003.

Burnett, John. "Legal Pot in the U.S. May Be Undercutting Mexican Marijuana." *National Public Radio.* Last modified December 2, 2014. http://www.npr.org/sections/parallels/2014/12/01/367802425/legal-pot-in-the-u-s-may-be-undercutting-mexican-marijuana.

Campbell, Greg. *Pot, Inc.: Inside Medical Marijuana, America's Most Outlaw Industry.* New York: Sterling, 2012.

Devinsky, Orrin, and Daniel Friedman. "We Need Proof on Marijuana." *New York Times,* February 12, 2014. http://www.nytimes.com/2014/02/13/opinion/we-need-proof-on-marijuana.html.

Haglage, Abby. "Life in Prison for Selling $20 of Weed." *Daily Beast,* February 27, 2015. http://www.thedailybeast.com/articles/2015/02/27/fate-vincent-winslow-got-life-in-prison-for-20-worth-of-weed.html.

Healy, Jack. "After 5 Months of Sales, Colorado Sees the Downside of a Legal High." *New York Times,* May 31, 2014. http://www.nytimes.com/2014/06/01/us/after-5-months-of -sales-colorado-sees-the-downside-of-a-legal-high.html.

——. "Legal Use of Marijuana Clashes with Job Rules." *New York Times,* September 7, 2014. http://www.nytimes.com/2014/09/08/us/legal-use-of-marijuana-clashes-with -workplace-drug-testing.html.

——. "New Scrutiny on Sweets with Ascent of Marijuana in Colorado." *New York Times,* October 29, 2014. http://www.nytimes.com/2014/10/30/us/new-scrutiny-on-sweets -with-ascent-of-marijuana-in-colorado.html.

Lee, Martin. *Smoke Signals: A Social History of Marijuana—Medical, Recreational, and Scientific.* New York: Scribner, 2012.

Martin, Alyson, and Nushin Rashidian. *A New Leaf: The End of Cannabis Prohibition.* New York: New Press, 2014.

Office of National Drug Control Policy. "Response to the New York Times Editorial Board's Call for Federal Marijuana Legalization." Whitehouse.gov. July 28, 2014. https://www .whitehouse.gov/blog/2014/07/28/response-new-york-times-editorial-marijuana -legalization.

Peikoff, Kira. "No Smoke, but Haze around E-Joint." *New York Times,* January 12, 2015. http:// www.nytimes.com/2015/01/13/health/with-the-e-joint-the-smoke-clears-.html.

Shortsleeve, Cassie. "The Truth about Medical Marijuana." *Men's Health,* April 20, 2013. http:// www.menshealth.com/medical-marijuana.

Sullivan Moore, Abigail. "This Is Your Brain on Drugs." *New York Times,* October 29, 2014. http://www.nytimes.com/2014/11/02/education/edlife/this-is-your-brain-on-drugs -marijuana-adults-teens.html.

Sullum, Jacob. "How Many Medical Marijuana Patients Are Fakers? Does It Matter?" *Reason. com*, August 5, 2011. http://reason.com/blog/2011/08/05/how-many-medical -marijuana-pat.

Further Information

Books

Alexander, Michelle. *The New Jim Crow: Mass Incarceration in the Age of Colorblindness.* New York: New Press, 2010.

Casarett, David. *Stoned: A Doctor's Case for Medical Marijuana.* New York: Current, 2015.

Fine, Doug. *Hemp Bound: Dispatches from the Front Lines of the Next Agricultural Revolution.* White River Junction, VT: Chelsea Green, 2014.

Hageseth, Christian. *Big Weed: An Entrepreneur's High-Stakes Adventures in the Budding Legal Marijuana Business.* New York: Palgrave Macmillan, 2015.

Hill, Kevin. *Marijuana: The Unbiased Truth about the World's Most Popular Weed.* Center City, MN: Hazelden, 2015.

Hiller, Catherine. *Just Say Yes: A Marijuana Memoir.* New York: Heliotrope, 2015.

Hillstrom, Kevin. *Medical Marijuana.* Farmington Hills, MI: Lucent, 2014.

Merino, Noel, ed. *Medical Marijuana.* Detroit: Greenhaven, 2011.

Ruschmann, Paul. *Legalizing Marijuana.* New York: Chelsea House, 2011.

Szumski, Bonnie, and Jill Karson. *Thinking Critically: Medical Marijuana.* San Diego: ReferencePoint, 2013.

Zott, Lynn. *Medical Marijuana.* Detroit: Greenhaven, 2012.

Websites

Americans for Safe Access (ASA)
http://www.safeaccessnow.org/
Americans for Safe Access works to ensure safe and legal access to medical marijuana for US patients as well as researchers. ASA's website offers information about marijuana for patients, health-care providers, and policy makers.

Drug Policy Alliance (DPA)
http://www.drugpolicy.org/
The Drug Policy Alliance is dedicated to reforming US drug laws, with an emphasis on reducing the harm created by both drug use and drug prohibition. The DPA website provides statistics about drug use and the War on Drugs; in-depth articles; and details on marijuana laws, marijuana use, and medical marijuana.

NORML
http://norml.org/
NORML is a leading voice for the reform of marijuana laws in the United States. It advocates for the legalization of marijuana for responsible adult use. The NORML website offers extensive information about marijuana and legalization efforts, with specific state-by-state details.

Office of National Drug Control Policy

https://www.whitehouse.gov/ondcp

The federal Office of National Drug Control Policy works to prevent drug use and abuse, funds scientific research on drug use, and attempts to expand access to treatment for drug users. The website includes details on specific drugs, including marijuana, and also discusses issues such as drugged driving and the abuse of prescription painkillers.

Partnership for Drug-Free Kids

http://www.drugfree.org/

Founded in 1987, the Partnership for Drug-Free Kids is dedicated to reducing substance abuse by teenagers and to supporting families impacted by drug addiction. The website offers information for teens and their parents. It talks about specific drugs, including marijuana, and issues such as the effects of drugs on the developing teenage brain.

Smart Approaches to Marijuana (SAM)

https://learnaboutsam.org/

Smart Approaches to Marijuana opposes the legalization and commercialization of marijuana. It seeks to educate the public about marijuana's harms and about problems created by marijuana legalization. The SAM website includes articles about marijuana and driving, marijuana and children, and marijuana and health.

Documentary Films

Clearing the Smoke: The Science of Cannabis. DVD. Bozeman: Montana PBS, 2011.
This documentary examines how cannabis acts on the human brain and body and evaluates its effectiveness in treating pain, nausea, seizures, and other ailments. The film features interviews with doctors, researchers, and medical marijuana patients.

Evergreen: The Road to Legalization. DVD. New York: First Run Features, 2013.
Starring Seattle-based travel writer and TV personality Rick Steves, *Evergreen* chronicles the political push to legalize recreational marijuana in the state of Washington, a campaign that achieved success in 2012.

The Other Side of Cannabis: Negative Effects of Marijuana on Our Youth. DVD. San Luis Obispo, CA: HeartsGate Productions, 2015.
Many health professionals believe that new, potent strains of marijuana can harm the developing brains of young people. This documentary examines recent research into the potential downsides of marijuana use.

Index

Photo Acknowledgments

The images in this book are used with the permission of: © underworld1/Bigstock.com, p. 1; © iStockphoto.com/Alberto Bogo (paper background); © iStockphoto.com/Boltenkoff (marijuana leaf); © iStockphoto.com/Adventure_Photo (green background), p. 3; AP Photo/Brennan Linsley, pp. 5, 58, 69; © Joe Amon/The Denver Post/Getty Images, p. 9; JASON REDMOND/REUTERS/Newscom, p. 12; © Science and Society/SuperStock, p. 15; Arthur Younger Ford (1861-1926) Photograph Albums, ULPA 1977.01.134, University of Louisville, p. 18; Library of Congress (LC-DIG-ds-00150), p. 19; Courtesy Everett Collection, p. 21; © Steven Clevenger/Corbis, p. 23; Courtesy Ronald Reagan Library, p. 27; AP Photo/DARRYL BUSH, p. 30; © Rod Rolle/Getty Images, p. 33; © Blaine Harrington III/Alamy, p. 39; © LANCE MURPHEY/The New York Times/Redux, p. 43; s_bukley/Newscom, p. 49; © Vika Sabo/Alamy, p. 54; © BSIP SA/Alamy, p. 56; © iStockphoto.com/pixdeluxe, p. 61; AP Photo/Patrick Reddy/The Kentucky Enquirer, p. 65; Marijuana Education Campaign created by the Colorado Department of Public Health and Environment in partnership with Cactus Communications, p. 74; AP Photo/ Cristophe Ena, p. 77; Werner R. Slocum/MCT/Newscom, p. 81; © PEOPLESTOCK/ Alamy, p. 87

Front jacket cover: © iStockphoto.com/Adventure_Photo (medical marijuana); © iStockphoto. com/Boltenkoff (marijuana leaf); back cover © underworld1/Bigstock.com; jacket flaps © iStockphoto.com/Alberto Bogo (paper background).

About the Author

Margaret J. Goldstein was born in Detroit and graduated from the University of Michigan. She and her dog, Jackie O, live in northern New Mexico. She has written and edited many books for young readers, including *Legalizing Drugs: Crime Stopper or Social Risk? Cyber Attack, America in the 1960s,* and the *Kirkus Reviews* star-reviewed *Fuel under Fire: Petroleum and Its Perils.*